The Star and the Sword

Israeli and Saudi involvement in the 9/11 attack

Wayne Madsen

ISBN: 978-1-312-45932-8

Table of Contents

Introduction

The presence in the United States of a number of young Israelis, most of whom had specialized military and intelligence backgrounds, in the months prior to 9/11 is a subject that received inadequate attention from the major U.S. media and government investigators. Many editors, bureau chiefs, and publishers either ignored the stories or spun them as nothing more than Israelis being caught working without proper U.S. visas.

Reporters who attempted to cover the Israeli/Saudi connection to 9/11 faced another problem. One senior reporter for the Associated Press recounted how his investigation into the Israeli "art student" story resulted in an Israel Lobby pressure group, CAMERA, or the Committee for Accuracy in Middle East Reporting in America, called his editor to complain a story written by the AP on the Israelis being arrested by U.S. authorities. If the pressure did not involve CAMERA, it took on the cloak of charging investigative reporters with being "anti-Semitic."

The activities of the Israelis fell into two main areas: the casing of the offices and homes of Federal law enforcement officials, U.S. military bases, and other sensitive sites by Israeli bogus "art students" during 2000 and 2001 and the unusual activities of Israeli furniture "movers" around sensitive areas during and after 9/11. These incidents occurred in tandem with the suspicious activities of other former Israeli military and intelligence officials in neighboring countries, including Canada and Mexico, after 9/11. In addition, a number of Israeli intelligence agents were apprehended abroad for passport violations and other illegal activities.

It is now been established that the art vending firms and furniture moving companies employing the Israelis were Israeli intelligence fronts.

The fact that the suspicious Israeli activity was directly linked to the movements of Al Qaeda cells in the United States could not be brushed aside as merely coincidental. For example, a number of the Israelis arrested for suspicious activities involving selling bogus Israeli art and driving moving vans were concentrated in the same neighborhoods where a number of the 9/11 Saudi hijackers lived and trained at flight schools. They used the same commercial mail box storefronts, video rental stores, and bars. In other words, the Israelis appeared to be keeping a close eye on the hijackers either as a support mechanism or a counter-terrorism shadowing operation.

A number of Israeli spokespersons and their corporate media apologists contended that the arrest of suspicious Israelis in the United States before and after 9/11 was no big thing.

What was ignored was the long history of Israeli espionage in America.

Although they were the subject to a multi-agency investigation for their links to Israeli intelligence, Israeli "art students" and mall kiosk vendors, who were extremely active in the United States in the months before and years after 9/11, have always maintained they are merely Israelis who want to travel and "see the world" after completing their military service. Practically every

Israeli working as door-to-door art salespeople and mall vendors are working in the United States illegally, violating their tourist visas.

After the detention of Israeli art students by U.S. authorities hit the media in early 2002, Mark Regev, the then-spokesman for the Israeli embassy in Washington and who later became Israeli Prime Minister Binyamin Netanyahu's spokesman, denied that any Israelis arrested in the United States were espionage agents. Regev categorically stated, "Israel does not spy on the United States," as if convicted American spy for Israel Jonathan Pollard never existed. Israeli sympathizers and propagandists within the U.S. corporate media all canted the same meme about the Israeli art students being spies: "It is an urban myth," they dutifully repeated *ad infinitum.*

However, in employment advertisements run in Israeli newspapers in 1979, it was quite clear that the hiring of Israeli students after their military service to subsequently be sent to the United States was a Mossad operation tied directly to the Israeli government. Those interested in Mossad spy work in the United States were directed to send their personal details to a post office box in Tel Aviv or the Israeli Consulate General in New York. The consulate is the largest Mossad station in the United States, with Washington, DC and Houston in second and third place.

Newspaper ad recruiting Israeli students for espionage work in the United States. Source: *Covert Action Information Bulletin*, **Dec. 1980.**

The advertisement read:

REQUIRED: STUDENTS TO WORK IN THE USA

Necessary Qualifications:

- Completion of military service in a combat unit (command position)
- Good health, profile 82 at least.

- Must be studying in the United States and/or planning to go there in Summer 1979 or beginning of 1980. Candidates must have been accepted at an educational institution in the United States.
- Candidate must pay travel expenses.
- Those interested should write and enclose a personal biography, personal information, identity card number.

In Israel: P.O. Box 39351, Tel Aviv (Attn: M.M.)

In U.S.A.: General Consulate/Israel in New York

800 Second Avenue, New York, NY 10017

---Only Qualified Persons Will Be Answered ---

Chapter 1 -- The Smoking Gun Documents

Two internal U.S. government documents that should not have been released to the public but were revealed that among the 120 Israeli "art students" who attempted to penetrate the security of dozens of Federal office buildings and visited the homes of scores of U.S. law enforcement personnel during 2000 and 2001 were some who used addresses and mail drops in southern Florida and Texas near those used by 9/11 hijackers. The information came from a Drug Enforcement Administration (DEA) Report drafted in June 2001 on the activities of the art students and a Federal Bureau of Investigation (FBI) list of the hijackers and other terrorist suspects, accidentally released in early October 2001 on a Finnish government web site. The DEA memo specifically stated that the Israelis may have had ties to an "Islamic fundamentalist group."

As a journalist, it became increasingly difficult from September 11, 2001 onward to cover the more secretive aspects of the U.S. intelligence and law enforcement communities. Many government officials have readopted the famous World War II missive of "Loose Lips Sink Ships," in refusing comment on anything deemed sensitive. Journalists who rely on the Freedom of Information Act to obtain copies of documents also faced unprecedented challenges.

After 9/11, Attorney General John Ashcroft issued a memorandum that stated his Justice Department would use its enormous legal might to defend any refusal by any government agencies to withhold information requested under the Freedom of Information Act.

Coming into possession of a sensitive Drug Enforcement Administration (DEA) report on the activities of Israeli "art students" was, therefore, a welcome surprise. DEA, the chief agency that investigates drug cartels, dangerous work under any circumstance, is traditionally very secretive about its investigations. However, some members of the agency, frustrated that their concerns were not being taken seriously by senior officials of the Federal Bureau of Investigation (FBI) and Justice Department, apparently decided to leak the report. Their decision was supported by the Immigration and Naturalization Service (INS), another agency involved with the DEA in the joint task force set up to investigate the Israeli "students."

Being presented with a document such as the DEA report, titled "Suspicious Activities Involving Israeli Art Students at DEA Facilities," poses unique problems in itself. For example, the document had to be verified as authentic and not a hoax. Many times, government agencies will merely state they "can neither confirm nor deny" the genuineness of leaked documents. However, in the case of the DEA report, confirmation of its genuineness came from the DEA in relatively quick fashion.

One amazing element of the story was the fact that a number of DEA, INS, and FBI agents discovered that several of the known addresses of the Israeli students were very close to those of the Al Qaeda terrorists and their supporters. These included addresses in Hollywood, Florida; Miami, Florida; and Irving, Texas. Speaking off-the-record, some of the agents told me that the fact that the Israelis and Al Qaeda were living in the same neighborhoods at the same time--January through May 2001--led the agents to believe the real mission of the Israelis was not to sell art at federal facilities but to spy on the Al Qaeda members.

As rock solid as the story about the true nature of the art students remains--it had to face another, even more insurmountable problem than getting federal agents to talk. Immediately after the story appeared in *Intelligence Online*, *Le Monde*, and the Associated Press, the sizeable pro-Israeli lobby in the United States began to gear up for a counter punch. They had been through this in December 2001 when the Fox News Network, in a four part series by Carl Cameron, referred to Israelis being arrested and detained in the United States for espionage. Cameron also stated, "Evidence linking these Israelis to 911 is classified. I cannot tell you about evidence that has been gathered. It's classified information." No sooner had Fox put the story on its web site it was pulled down without explanation. A similar story on Houston's CBS affiliate, KHOU-TV, provided the following introduction:

> "10/02/2001 - Fifteen People Arrested in March in Dallas, Suspected of Casing Federal Buildings. 11News reported how people claiming to be "Israeli art students" might be trying to sneak into federal buildings and defense sites, and even doing surveillance. In Dallas, the so-called students hit early this year at the city's FBI building, the Drug Enforcement Administration and at the Earle

Cabell Federal building, where guards found one student wandering the halls with a floor plan of the building."[1]

When trying to access the full story on the TV station's web site, one receives the following message: "The page you requested could not be found." However, Channel 11 News' terrorism expert and former Defense Department analyst Ron Hatchett said the Israeli activity was "obvious surveillance" and "not a bunch of kids selling artwork." A Federal Protective Service memo, obtained by KHOU after Israelis were seen casing the Leland Federal office building in Houston, stated, "Federal sites have experienced an inundation of art solicitations at office buildings by students claiming to be selling Israeli art."[2]

Federal agents in Dallas were also concerned that the Israeli art students had other intentions. The office manager for a Plano physician reported that after being told to leave, the Israelis kept returning to her building, which had a no soliciting policy. Channel 8 in Dallas reported that a number of Israelis were caught casing Federal buildings in Dallas and being involved in suspicious behavior in north Texas.[3]

The author's own colleagues reported that aggressive Israeli art students paid visits during late 2000 and early 2001 to the offices of the

[1] Anna Werner, "Federal Buildings Could Be In Jeopardy - In Houston and Nationally; Government guards have found so-called students trying to get into secure buildings, KHOU-TV 11 News, October 1, 2001.
[2] Ibid.
[3] Brett Shipp, "News 8 Investigates 'Art Students,'" October 3, 2001.

Electronic Privacy Information Center (EPIC) in Washington, DC and the headquarters of the National Defense Industrial Association (NDIA) in Arlington, Virginia.

Other suspected Israeli intelligence activity surrounding 911, including the arrest by New Jersey police near Giants Stadium of five Israelis who were seen celebrating, high-fiving, jumping up and down, and videotaping the collapse of the World Trade Center, was reported by the media. A New Jersey apartment resident named Maria, who declined to give her last name, told ABC News about several Israelis she saw celebrating the attack on the Twin Towers in her parking lot. The Israelis were later linked to an Israeli-owned office moving company called Urban Moving Systems headquartered in Weehawken, New Jersey at 3 West 18th Street. Another Urban Moving office was located on West 50th Street in Manhattan. Urban Moving's owner, Dominik Otto Suter, fled to Israel on September 14, shortly before he was to be re-questioned by the FBI. [4] One of the five Israelis had a ticket for Bangkok and was due to fly out on September 13.[5] The New York Department of Transportation revoked Urban Moving Systems' license after it was discovered that its Manhattan business address was merely a post office box. Suter's name turned

---

[4] Neil Mackay, "Five Israelis were seen filming from the van on the right as jet liners ploughed into the Twin Towers on September 11, 2001. Were they part of a massive spy ring which shadowed the 911 hijackers and knew that al-Qaeda planned a devastating terrorist attack on the USA?" *Sunday Herald*, November 2, 2003, p. 1.

[5] Jim Galloway, "Innocent Israelis Caught Up in Arrests," *Palm Beach Post*, November 18, 2001, p. 21A.

up on a "Law Enforcement Sensitive" FBI suspect list of individuals and companies suspected of involvement in the 9-11 attacks. Suter's year of birth is listed as 1970 with a social security number of 129-78-0926. His addresses on 9-11 is listed as 28 Harlow Crescent Rd., Fairlawn, NJ 07410. Previous addresses are listed as 312 Pavonia Ave., Jersey City, NJ 07302; and 15000 Dickens, Suite 11, Sherman Oaks CA.[6]

At 3:31 P.M. the FBI issued a nationwide alert called "Be On Lookout" or "BOLO" for the Israelis. Drafted by Special Agent Dave O'Brien, it read:

"Vehicle possibly related to New York terrorist attack. White, 2000 Chevrolet van with New Jersey registration (JYJ 13Y) with 'Urban Moving Systems' sign on back seen at Liberty State Park. Jersey City, NJ, at the time of the first impact of jetliner into World Trade Center."[7]

According to FBI sources, Urban Moving Systems and the activities of its employees on 911 did not sit too well with one member of the FBI's New York Joint Terrorism Task Force, Special Agent Michael Dick. Dick, a colleague of former FBI Counter-terrorism division chief John O'Neill, aggressively investigated this Israeli ring before and after 911. But like O'Neill, he soon found himself removed from his duties on the orders of the then-head of the Justice Department's Criminal Division Michael Chertoff. Dick was very suspicious when Israeli movers

---

[6] FBI Suspect List, dated May 22, 2002.
[7] Information from East Rutherford Police Department.

14

quickly moved Zim American Israeli Shipping Company out of its 10,000 square feet of office space on the 17th Floor of the North Tower of the World Trade Center. The partially Israeli state-owned firm forfeited a $50,000 security deposit when it terminated its lease and vacated the building one week prior to 911. According to a non-official cover (NOC) CIA source who worked with Dick, Israeli movers moved explosives into the 17th Floor office space after Zim moved out.[8]

Dick pursued the Israeli angle but soon found himself transferred to Karachi, Pakistan to help rescue *Wall Street Journal* reporter Daniel Pearl who had been kidnapped by Al Qaeda functionaries. There was one hitch. The FBI was already aware that Pearl had been brutally murdered by his captors.

Urban Moving Systems Weehawken, NJ bomb making and anthrax storage warehouse.

---

[8] October 2, 2005, "Clearing the Baffles for 9/11," WayneMadsenReport.com

Moments after Maria felt the ground shake from the impact of the first plane into the World Trade Center and she received a phone call from a neighbor to look out her window at the southern Manhattan skyline, she noticed a white Chevy van parked in the lower parking lot with three of the five men in the van jumping on the roof of the vehicle and videotaping each other with the carnage in the background. Maria was also shocked that the men were celebrating the horrific scenes across the Hudson River. After writing down the license plate number of the van, Maria and her husband Pat phoned the police.[9]

Subsequently, Information Spectrum, Inc. (ISI) of Cherry Hill, New Jersey, a subsidiary of the Fairfax, Virginia-based defense contractor, Anteon, took over the operation of the Jersey City police computer system that handled all incoming emergency phone calls on September 11. The system had been maintained by Larimore Associates, a company that specializes in archiving police emergency calls. However, Larimore's contract was abruptly canceled by Jersey City authorities and awarded to Information Spectrum after the sudden death from a heart attack of Jersey City's first African-American mayor, Democrat, Glenn D. Cunningham, himself a former Jersey City police officer. According to Jersey City Police officials, after the emergency call system was changed from Wang to a Windows environment, 8000 emergency 911

---

[9] John Miller, "Five Israeli men arrested soon after 911 might have been working for Israeli intelligence, but likely did not know beforehand about the attacks," ABC News, 20/20, June 21, 2002.

16

system calls registered on September 11were scrubbed from the archives. In fact, archives dating back to 1989, including those dealing with the 1993 bombing of the World Trade Center, were similarly affected. Information Spectrum's running of the computer system resulted in a number of server crashes. When Larimore volunteered to help recover lost data, there was no answer from the police department.[10] Some Jersey City police sources speculated the change from Larimore to ISI/Anteon was prompted by orders from Trenton and the administration of Governor James McGreevey. They termed the changeover as "political." Governor McGreevey resigned in 2004 after it was discovered he had an alleged gay relationship with his chief of Homeland Security, Golan Cipel. An Israeli citizen, Cipel, a former diplomat assigned to Israel's Consulate General in New York City, was thought by many intelligence experts to be a junior Mossad case officer who lured McGreevey into a "honey trap."

Adding insult to injury, it was later revealed that Urban Moving Systems had received a grant from the federal government. In 2001, the Mossad front received $498,750 in assistance from the U.S. federal government, according to FedSpending.org, a web site operated by the federal spending watchdog organization, OMB Watch.[11] There was never any explanation given by the government for why a known Mossad front received nearly a half million dollars of taxpayers'

---

[10] Confidential source, Larimore Associates.

[11] June 20-22, 2008, "U.S. government funded Mossad 9/11-related moving firm," WayneMadsenReport.com

money. Later, the website curiously removed the entry from its database.

Assistance to URBAN MOVING SYSTEMS INC in NJ (FY 2000-2006)

List of Recipients for FY 2001

You can click on the column headers below to re-sort the search.

Recipient Name	State	Federal Funding (for this search)
URBAN MOVING SYSTEMS INC	New Jersey	**$498,750**

Total recipients for fiscal year 2001: 1

Federal funding (within this search) for the year: $498,750
Further information from OMB Watch's Federal Spending website, indicates that in addition to the $498,750 Israeli Mossad front Urban Moving Systems received in June 2001 from the Small Business Administration (SBA), it also received $166,250 from "non-federal funding."

Suter's name appeared on a terrorist watchlist provided by the FBI and leaked by Italian financial surveillance authorities. His name appears along with all the 9/11 Arab hijackers. A similar list, also based on FBI information, and leaked by the Finnish financial surveillance authority, did not contain Suter's name.

The list from Italy contains the following addresses for Suter:

18

- 28 Harlow Crescent Rd. Fair Lawn, NJ 07410;
- 312 Pavonia Ave. Jersey City, NJ 07302;
- 15000 Dickens Suite 11 Sherman Oaks, CA

A year of birth of 1970 and a Social Security Number of 129-78-0926 is also listed.

A Veromi search resulted in a full name for Suter of Dominick Otto Suter, with addresses in Fairlawn, New Jersey; Jersey City, NJ; and New York City. Weehawaken is listed as the business address for Urban Moving Systems. Another Veromi search resulted in New Rochelle, New York as another business address for Urban Moving Systems, a total of four addresses for the firm before 9/11: New York City, Bayonne, Weehawken, and New Rochelle.

Veromi also listed Ornit Levinson as a possible relative of Suter's with addresses in New York City, Fairlawn, NJ, Jersey City, Sherman Oaks, California, New Rochelle, and Van Nuys, California. Two businesses are associated with Levinson: 1 Stop Cleaning LLC of Royal Palm Beach and Wellington, Florida and INVSUPPORT, Inc. of Wellington, Florida. The Italian watchlist also lists Omit Levinson, aka Omit Suter, with a birth year of 1971 and a Social Security Number of 122-78-0232. Addresses for Levinson are listed as:

- 28 Harlow Crescent Rd., Fairlawn, NJ 07410
- 312 Pavonia Ave.,Jersey City, NJ 07302
- 15000 Dickens Ste 11, Sherman Oaks, CA

The Florida Articles of Incorporation for INVSUPPORT lists Levinson as director with an address of 11924 Forest Hill Blvd., Suite 22, #372, Wellington, Florida 33414. The state of New Jersey filed a civil suit against Suter and Urban Moving Systems in Florida in 2005. A West Palm Beach, Florida address is listed for Suter.

Assistance to URBAN MOVING SYSTEMS INC in NJ
(FY 2001)

Expanded Detail on Individual Transactions for FY 2001

Award Or Aggregate #1

Recipient Information

Recipient Name	URBAN MOVING SYSTEMS INC
Recipient City Name	BAYONNE
Recipient County Name	HUDSON
Recipient State Code	New Jersey
Recipient Zip Code	07002
Congressional District	NJ90: New Jersey unknown districts
Recipient Category	Individuals
Recipient Type	individual

Project and Award Info

Major Agency	Small Business Administration
Agency Code	7300: Small Business Administration

Agency Name SMALL BUSINESS ADMINISTRATION

Federal Award ID 45966540

State

Application ID Number SAI EXEMPT

CFDA Program Number 59.012: Small Business Loans

CFDA Program Title SMALL BUSINESS LOANS

Assistance Category Loans (both direct and guaranteed)

Assistance Type guaranteed/insured loan

Project Description TO AID SMALL BUSINESSES WHICH ARE UNABLE TO OBTAIN FINANCING IN THE PRIVATE CREDIT MARKETPLACE

Action   (Award or Aggregate #1)

Fiscal Year	2001
Action Type	new assistance action
Federal Funding Amount	$498,750 *
Non-Federal Funding Amount	$166,250
Total Funding Amount	$665,000
Obligation / Action Date	06/22/2001
Starting Date	06/22/2001
Ending Date	06/22/2024
Record Type	individual action

* Note: The Small Business Administration appears to include loans that have been authorized but for which no disbursement of funding was made in their spending data that is reported to the U.S. Census Bureau. We have alerted SBA of this problem in its data and are working with them to resolve it.

Principal Place
Principal Place Code   3403580
Principal Place State   NEW JERSEY
Principal Place County or City BAYONNE

There was never a full federal law enforcement investigation of Urban Moving Systems.

Chapter 2 -- The Saudi drug smuggling connection to 9/11

It is significant that the DEA was the first federal agency to suspect the Israeli "art students" as individuals involved in more than narcotics smuggling. There are also significant connections between the government of Saudi Arabia and 9/11, links also discovered by the DEA.

In 1999, the DEA broke open a major conspiracy involving a Saudi prince's Colombian cocaine smuggling from Venezuela to support some "future intention" involving Koranic prophecy. The DEA operations were contained in a "Declassification of a Secret DEA 6 Paris Country Office" memorandum dated June 26, 2000, a date which coincided with the height of Israeli art student and 911 hijacker activity in the United States. In June 1999, 808 kilograms of cocaine were seized in Paris. At the same time, the DEA was conducting a major investigation of the Medellin drug cartel called OPERATION MILLENNIUM.

Through an intercepted fax, the Bogota Country Office of the DEA learned of the Paris cocaine seizure and linked the drug smuggling operation to the Saudis. The DEA investigation centered around Saudi Prince Nayif al Saud, whose alias was El Principe (the Prince). Nayif's full name is Nayif (or Nayef) bin Fawwaz al-Shaalan al-Saud. In pursuit of his international drug deals, Nayif traveled in his own Boeing 727 and used his diplomatic status to avoid customs checks. The DEA report stated Nayif studied at the University of Miami, Florida, owned a bank in Switzerland, speaks eight languages, was heavily invested in Venezuela's petroleum industry, regularly visited the United States, and traveled with millions of dollars of U.S. currency. Nayif was also invested in Colombia's petroleum industry.

Nayif was also reported to have met with drug cartel members in Marbella, Spain, where the late Saudi King Fahd and the Saudi royal family maintained a huge palatial residence. The report states that when a group of cartel members traveled to Riyadh to meet Nayif, "they were picked up in a Rolls Royce automobile belonging to Nayif, and driven to the Riyadh Holiday Inn hotel. The next day they were met by Nayif and his brother [believed to be named Saul [sic] [His twin brother is Prince Saud. Nayif's older brother, Prince Nawaf, is married to King Abdullah's daughter].)… The second day they all traveled to the desert in terrain vehicles [hummers]. During this desert trip they discussed narcotics trafficking. UN [The DEA informant] and Nayif agreed to conduct the 2,000 kilogram cocaine shipment, which would be delivered to Caracas, VZ, by UN's people, where Nayif would facilitate the cocaine's transport to Paris, France. Nayif explained he would utilize his 727 jet airliner, under Diplomatic cover, to transport the cocaine. The Boeing 727 was operated by Skyways

International, a Saudi-owned airline with past connections to the mysterious James Bath, George W. Bush's Texas Air National Guard friend and later Arbusto and Harken Energy investment pass-through between the Saudis and Bush. These investors included Salem Bin Laden, Osama Bin Laden's late older brother who was killed in a 1988 plane crash in Texas. Bath was the registered agent for Salem Bin Laden.

Nayif told "UN" that he could transport up to 20,000 kilograms of cocaine in his jet airliner, and propositioned "UN" to "conduct 10-20,000 kilogram shipments in the future."

"UN" wondered why Nayif, supposedly a devout Muslim, would be involved with drugs. Nayif's response in light of what is now known about Saudi funding of terrorism, is worth a close perusal. During the Riyadh meeting, Nayif responded to "UN's" question by stating that "he is a strict advocate of the Muslim Corran [sic]." "UN" stated, "Nayif does not drink, smoke, or violate any of the Corran's [sic] teachings. "UN" asked Nayif why he [Nayif] wanted to sell cocaine and Nayif stated that the world is already doomed and that he has been authorized by God to sell drugs. Nayif stated that "UN" would later learn of Nayif's true intentions for trafficking narcotics although Nayif would not comment further." The Saudi prince's drug smuggling operation was smashed by the DEA and French police in October 1999.[12]

---

[12] Drug Enforcement Administration, Memorandum, Declassification of Secret DEA 6 for Paris Country Office, June 26, 2000.

On May 16, 1999, Prince Nayif's Skyways Boeing 727 touched down at LeBourget Airport outside of Paris (this is the same airport that received the Bin Laden family flight from the United States following the 9/11 attacks). Also on board the plane were a number of Saudi princes and princesses. Two tons of cocaine, smuggled on to the aircraft in Caracas, were transported as one large diplomatic pouch by two waiting Saudi vans. The cocaine was transported to Noissy-le-Sec, a Paris suburb. A French-US law enforcement case against Nayif and his entourage, complete with evidence and confidential informants soon collapsed.

A "Confidential Diplomatic" cable from the French embassy in Saudi Arabia to Paris warning that Saudi Interior Minister Prince Nayef had warned that if France pursued the case against the Saudi prince, a lucrative €7 billion radar defense contract, Project SBGDP (*Garde Frontiere*), with the French firm Thales would be canceled. The embassy cable sought pressure against the French Interior Ministry to drop its investigation of Nayif. The cable also indicated that Saudi Interior Minister Nayef's irritation at the French investigation was shared by his brothers Abdullah (then-Crown Prince) and Sultan (Defense Minister) as well as the Governor of Riyadh Province Prince Salman. Saudi informers have revealed that Al Qaeda members routinely traveled through Riyadh on their way to Pakistan and then to Taliban Afghanistan. These insiders report that Salman's office arranged for cash payments, hotels, and air fares for the Al Qaeda members.

The French cable also states that the Saudis reiterated that it was merciless to drug traffickers for which Saudi youth were often the victims. The Saudis also told the French that unlike Afghanistan, Pakistan, Egypt, Syria, and Lebanon, Saudi Arabia was not a base for drug trafficking. The reaction by the Saudi government's key principals to the French drug investigation indicates they had something to hide. Perhaps similar to the Bush family, they had an off-the-books operation to generate hundreds of millions of dollars for their Wahhabi compatriots in Afghanistan and Pakistan, including the Taliban and Al Qaeda. The French cable draws attention to intelligence rumors that the cocaine transported by Nayif from Venezuela originated in Colombia -- the same country from where George H. W. Bush and his Iran-contra co-conspirators arranged for cocaine-for-cash-for-weapons transfers involving Panamanian dictator Manuel Noriega as a middleman. CIA sources have recently reported that lead hijacker Mohammed Atta was known to U.S., British, and Saudi intelligence as a heroin courier from Mujaheddin-controlled Afghanistan as early as 1991. Atta was also identified as a cocaine user. Hence, what the French and U.S. law enforcement investigators discovered in 1999 may have been a major financial source for Al Qaeda's terrorist attacks. Recent revelations that a Top Secret U.S. Special Operations Command/Defense Intelligence Agency unit code named Able Danger was shadowing Al Qaeda operatives in 1999, the same year that Nayif and his courier activities were discovered, indicates high level collusion inside the United States Defense and Justice Departments with elements that did not want to embarrass the Saudis. As with the DEA investigation of Nayif, Able Danger was shut down on orders by Pentagon lawyers.

It was quite possible that the massive amounts of Able Danger data reported to have been destroyed on the Atta team may have included gigabytes of financial data on Prince Nayif's drug money laundering activities. A European intelligence agency flow chart titled "OPERATION PALME" illustrated the connections of Nayif's brother Nawwaf's financial operations to a myriad of other entities, a large number of them based in Geneva, a city hosting a number of Bush-connected entities tied to the 9/11 attacks, including a money transfer to at least one of the hijackers.

French Confidential Cable

According to the Operation Palme chart, Nawwaf bin Fawwaz al-Shaalan is Vice President of Kanz Bank located at 65 rue du Rhone in Geneva. This bank is linked to Bammer Financial Trade Organization at 7 rue Versonnex in Geneva, Virgin Corporation LLC in Vessy (Geneva Canton), Maison Virgin Corporation also in Vessy, Degroof Luxembourg SA of Genf, Geneva Canton, and Capital Trust SA, 640 Avenida Diagonal, Barcelona, Spain.

A business card shows a clear link between Skyways International, the firm tied to the Bush family and the Saudis, and the National Commercial Bank of Saudi Arabia. The business card for a flight engineer named Keith Monroe indicates that Skyways International is a subsidiary of the National Commercial Bank.

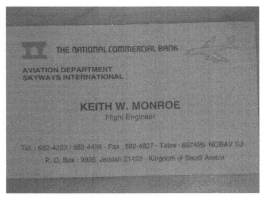

National Commercial Bank-Skyways Connection

In 1992, according to *The Houston Chronicle*, George W. Bush's friend James Bath was investigated by the Treasury Department's Financial Crimes Enforcement Network

(FINCEN) and the FBI. Investigators suspected Saudi investors who worked with Bath of illegally trying to influence U.S. policy during the Reagan and Bush I administrations. Bath invested Saudi money in Arbusto '70 Ltd., Arbusto '80 Ltd., and Bush Exploration Co. (which later morphed into Harken Energy Corp., which included George W. Bush as its director). After Desert Storm, Harken was granted lucrative off-shore drilling rights by Bahrain, a Desert Storm coalition partner. One of the other shareholders of Harken, along with Bush, was Saudi businessman Abdullah Taha Bakhsh. According to the *Chronicle*, Bath, who was a sole agent of Salem Bin Laden, was also the sole director of Skyway Aircraft Leasing Corp., one of the affiliates of Skyways International. Bath established four corporate entities with the name "Skyway" and the firm that incorporated the corporate contrivances in the Cayman Islands for Bath was the same one that established a Cayman-based money laundering front company for Oliver North in the Iran-contra scandal. In 1977, Bath bought Houston Gulf Airport on behalf of Salem Bin Laden. Skyway Aircraft Leasing Corporation was, according to the *Chronicle*, owned by Khalid Bin Mahfouz, a major shareholder in the defunct Bank of Credit and Commerce International (BCCI), a major money laundering activity for George H. W. Bush's Iran-contra caper. Bin Mahfouz was also the owner of the National Commercial Bank of Saudi Arabia.[13]

------

[13] Jerry Urban, "Feds Investigate Entrepreneur Allegedly Tied to Saudis," *The Houston Chronicle*, June 3, 1992.

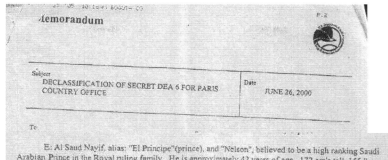

Memorandum

Subject	Date
DECLASSIFICATION OF SECRET DEA 6 FOR PARIS COUNTRY OFFICE	JUNE 26, 2000

To:

E: Al Saud Nayif, alias: "El Principe"(prince), and "Nelson"; believed to be a high ranking Saudi Arabian Prince in the Royal ruling family. He is approximately 42 years of age, 172 cm's tall, 155 lbs. Has a twin brother named Saul. Travels under Diplomatic status in his own 727 jetliner. Studied at the University of Miami, in Miami, Fl. Speaks eight (8) languages. Owns a bank in Switzerland. Possibly has a child with Doris Salazar. Has major investment in the petroleum business in Venezuela. Travels with millions of dollars of U.S. currency. Regularly visits the U.S.

DEA Report on Saudi drug smuggling

There has never been any explanation by the Saudis of what Prince Nayif's ultimate intentions were and what he was planning to do with the cash from the illegal cocaine shipments. In light of the funding for 911 and other terrorist incidents, the DEA report on OPERATION MILLENNIUM takes on greater significance. Did Saudi drug smuggling proceeds help pay for the 911 attack? Why was this possible connection overlooked by the 911 Commission? What did the Able Danger team stumble across while Nayif was smuggling drugs? Was Atta a part of this Saudi drug network? If so, why was Atta, a drug courier, permitted to enter the United States on numerous occasions?

It would appear that the Saudis, in connection with people closely associated with George W. Bush (perhaps including Bush himself as well as his father), have been giving a "wink and a nod" to illicit airline smuggling businesses involving drugs and money laundering for a number of years. There are American citizens currently sitting in prisons under mandatory harsh drug-related sentences for doing much less than what the Bush crime family, their Saudi partners, and their network of drug mules and couriers (including Mohammed Atta and Saudi Prince Nayif) have been getting away with for decades. The Racketeer Influenced and Corrupt Organization (RICO) statutes cry out for an accounting by these individuals before a court of law.

According to well-informed police sources in New Jersey, on the evening of September 10, 2001, the four men who would, the following morning, hijack United Flight 93 en route from Newark Liberty International Airport to San Francisco, were living it up at a Wayne, New Jersey strip club called "Lace."

The four hijackers, Ziad Jarrah (Lebanese), the pilot, and three Saudis: Ahmed al-Haznawi, Ahmed al-Nami, and Saeed al-Ghamdi were later pegged by U.S. authorities as extreme Wahhabi Muslim followers of Osama bin Laden. However, the security videotape from "Lace" showed the four to be far from pious followers of Wahhabism. In what seemingly appears to be an attempt by the Bush administration to keep the myth alive that the hijackers were fanatic Muslims, the FBI confiscated the security tape from "Lace" and it was never identified or discussed in the official 911 Commission report. That security video tape joins a number of others -- including those from the area around the Pentagon showing the impact of American Airlines 77 into the building and a Jersey City video rental store across Kennedy Boulevard from the El Salaam Mosque -- that have been confiscated by the FBI. The El Salaam

Mosque is where both the 1993 and 2001 World Trade Center attackers were active prior to each attack. The Kennedy Boulevard video store video tapes showing Saudi hijackers and Israeli Urban Moving Systems Israeli agents patronizing the store were seized as evidence by the FBI and the store's computer hard drive, with the names, addresses, and phone numbers of video rental customers, was stolen in a "black bag" operation believed to have been carried out by the FBI.[14]

The dots began to rapidly connect with the release of FBI documents on post-9/11 Saudi-chartered flights from the United States. The documents were released to Judicial Watch pursuant to a Freedom of Information Act request. The documents described a number of charter flights flying Saudis out of the United States in the immediate aftermath of 9/11, including Saudi royal family and Bin Laden family members. There is even the tantalizing possibility that Osama Bin Laden, himself, chartered some of the flights that spirited his family members out of the United States.

Particular interest was focused on one document describing a Saudi charter flight aboard a Gabon-flagged aircraft, a DC-8-73, tail number TR-LTZ, which departed La Vegas on September 19, 2001 bound for Geneva, Switzerland. On September 11 and 12, the Saudis, all reputedly members of the royal family, were staying at the Four Seasons Hotel and Caesar's Palace in Las Vegas.

The Associated Press reported on September 26, 2001 that the FBI took possession

---

[14] September 11, 2006 report, WayneMadsenReport.com

of photographs and other documents from SunCruz Casino boats, owned by jailed GOP lobbyist and Israeli Lobby kingpin Jack Abramoff. The report stated, "SunCruz Casinos has turned over photographs and other documents to FBI investigators after employees said they recognized some of the men suspected in the terrorist attacks as customers. Names on the passenger list from a Sept. 5 cruise matched those of some of the hijackers. Two or three men linked to the Sept. 11 hijackings may have been customers on a ship that sailed from Madeira Beach on Florida's Gulf Coast."

Florida investigative journalist Daniel Hopsicker later learned that one of those on board the casino boat was Mohammed Atta, the alleged chief hijacker. Abramoff took over control of Sun Cruz from Gus Boulis, who was gunned down gangland-style on a Fort Lauderdale street on February 6, 2001.

Saudi royals are allegedly Wahhabi Muslims who eschew such "decadent" places as casinos and bars. The presence of Saudis in Vegas and Atta on a gambling boat in Florida paints a much different picture. It was known that United Flight 93 hijackers were present on the evening of September 10, 2001, in a Wayne, New Jersey strip club before rising in the morning and heading off to Newark International Airport.

Abramoff, at the time of the Gabonese charter flight, was one of that oil-rich nation's chief lobbyists in Washington. Abramoff's connections with the Saudis and African nations, such as Gabon, go back to the 1980s when he and GOP right-wing activist Grover Norquist, who now has close links to the Saudis, were aiding

Afghan mujaheddin guerrillas via their International Freedom Foundation (IFF), which once held a summit of anti-communist rebels from Afghanistan, Laos, Nicaragua, and Angola in the Angolan jungle headquarters of Jonas Savimbi's UNITA faction. Gabon's President, Omar Bongo, a convert to Islam, was a close ally of the Saudis. Bongo and Savimbi also had a mutual friend -- Abramoff. IFF was also supported by a number of right-wing groups in the United States and the government of apartheid South Africa. IFF also had the backing of two other nations that might, at first, appear diametrically opposed to one another -- Israel and Saudi Arabia.

The Israeli-Saudi links not only developed after their cooperation in support of the Afghan mujaheddin and other anti-communist rebels but flourished.

There were already links between Saudi intelligence and the Mossad through the Safari Club, a secret intelligence-sharing alliance signed on September 1, 1976, between Sheikh Kamal Addam, the Turkish-born head of Saudi intelligence; General Nemotollah Nassiri, the head of Iran's SAVAK; and the heads of Egyptian and Moroccan intelligence. The Safari Club had the support of the British, French, and Turkish intelligence services, as well as the CIA, then headed by George H. W. Bush.

Addam secretly arranged in the behind-the-scenes work for Egyptian President Anwar Sadat's visit to Jerusalem to meet Israeli Prime Minister Menachem Begin in 1977. Some radical Saudi royals were incensed by this and Addam was replaced by Prince Turki, the future liaison man between the Saudi royals and Osama Bin Laden.

In 1985, Saudi Arabia wanted to buy sophisticated AWACS planes from the United States. The Israeli Lobby did not want the Reagan administration to sell such aircraft to the Saudis, not because they mistrusted their Saudi royal friends but because they considered the Saudi regime unstable and were afraid the planes could end up in the hands of a Saddam Hussein, Hafez Assad, or a nationalist, anti-Western regime in Saudi Arabia.

However, the Israelis raised no objections when a parallel arms deal was made between Saudi Arabia and Britain to buy sophisticated weapons, including jet fighters. That deal was known as the Yamamah deal with BAE Systems. The British media is now reporting on alleged bribes paid by BAE to Saudi ambassador to the United States Prince Bandar. Yearly payments of $100 million were allegedly paid to Bandar through Riggs Bank in Washington, a bank with which the Bush family had close ties. Prince Turki also reportedly received British payments.

Bandar's wife, Prince Haifa, used money from the same Riggs accounts containing the secret payments, to pay for the lodging of one of the 9/11 hijackers.

The Yamamah deal was reportedly overseen by Charles Powell (now Lord Charles Powell), a close adviser to then-British Prime Minister Margaret Thatcher. Powell's brother, Jonathan Powell, is the chief of staff to Prime Minister Tony Blair. Another brother, Hugh Powell, is the chief of security for the British Foreign Office. The Powells ensured that the

Thatcher-John Major-Tony Blair transitions ensured the secrecy of the BAE payments to the Saudis, payments that later expanded to include post-apartheid South African officials and Czech government leaders.

Lord Charles Powell became an adviser to the board of BAE and he also served on the board of Jardine Matheson, a Hong Kong-based business empire that is linked to HSBC, the Hong Kong and Shanghai Banking Corporation, which reportedly was involved in the transfer of funds through Dubai to pay the 9/11 hijackers in the United States. In fact, Treasury Secretary Paul O'Neill was fired by the Bush administration after he pressured Dubai and Saudi officials about the laundering of terrorist money through banks under their control.

After 9/11, O'Neill attempted to pressure banks and other financial institutions in Dubai and Saudi Arabia to provide records of past and ongoing Al Qaeda financial transactions. According to a former auditor with the Central Bank of the United Arab Emirates, during a trip by O'Neill in March 2002, the UAE and Saudi officials shook O'Neill's hand, smiled at him, and offered to assist. However, they soon put pressure on the Bush administration, including several leading neo-cons who knew the stakes of such disclosures, to force Paul O'Neill out. Later that year, in December, Bush forced O'Neill to resign. A November 29, 2001 letter from Treasury Department General Counsel David D. Aufhauser to Swiss Procurator General Claude Nicati described the measures the Treasury Department was taking against a major Al Qaeda financier named Yassin A. Kadi. However, that particular thread intersected with activities by Islamist guerrillas in Bosnia, and that was a threat to certain neocon elements who had established a Bosnian support fund in the 1990s that involved the same financial support networks that supported Al Qaeda. In fact, Al Qaeda units were active in Bosnia during the civil war. And those units were partly supported by the Bosnia Defense Fund established by two leading neo-conservatives championing American wars with Muslim nations, Richard Perle and Douglas Feith. The latter was known to U.S. counterintelligence as having close relations with a number of Mossad officials in Washington, DC, Jerusalem, and Tel Aviv.

According to the Aufhauser letter to his Swiss counterpart, "Mr. Kadi has acknowledged in a number of press accounts that he is the founder of the Muwafaq, or 'Blessed Relief' Foundation. He is identified in legal records as 'Chairman' of the foundation. The leader of the terrorist organization Al-Gama'at Al-Islamiya, Tala Fuad Kassem, has said that the Muwafaq Foundation provided logistical and financial support for a mujahadin battalion in Bosnia. The foundation also operated in Sudan, Somalia, and Pakistan, among other places." The letter continued, "Muhammad Ali Harrath, main activist of the Tunisian Islamic Front (TIF) in the United Kingdom, was associated with Muwafaq personnel in Bosnia and other TIF members worked at the Muwafaq Foundation."[15]

The facts strongly indicated that there was high-level coordination between Abramoff's

---

[15] October 2, 2005, "Clearing the Baffles for 9/11," WayneMadsenReport.com

underworld network of Russian-Ukrainian-Israeli gangsters, wealthy Saudi financiers, and neocon operatives within the Bush administration to bring about a U.S. military invasion of Iraq, to be followed by an attack on Iran. The over 200 so-called Israeli "art students" who were living among the 9/11 hijackers in the months before 9/11 were creating diversions for federal law enforcement. The Israeli "movers" who confused law enforcement on the morning of 9/11 continued the diversionary "false flag" tactics. There are two nations in the Middle East that lacked the ability to take on Baghdad and Tehran -- and they are the two that have left indelible fingerprints on the attacks of 9/11: Israel and Saudi Arabia. And they and their surrogates in the United States had an interest in luring the United States into bloody Middle East war and almost 7000 American civilians and military members have paid for this treachery with their lives.[16]

---

[16] June 21, 2007, "Jack Abramoff's major client surfaces in post-9/11 Air Bin Laden' flights from US," WayneMadsenReport.com

Chapter 3 -- The "Dancing Israelis"

Jersey City was a major base of operations for the 1993 World Trade Center attack. The Ryder van used in that attack was rented from a Jersey City rental agency. As for the 9/11 attacks on the World Trade Center, there were no records of a call by Maria or any other witness to the Israeli activity in Maria's building parking lot or at Liberty State Park. The only call remaining in the system was a late night call on September 11 about a suspicious vagrant in a south Jersey City neighborhood.[17]

However, there was a call placed to the Jersey City Police Department that claimed "Palestinians" in Arab clothes were seen celebrating the attacks. Although the Jersey City Police discovered their 911 system tapes on September 11, 2001 disappeared from their servers and archives after ISI took over the contract, some tapes implicating "Arabs" found their way into the hands of WNBC-TV in New York in June 2002. WNBC played transcripts of 911 calls from the Jersey City Police:

Dispatcher: Jersey City police.
Caller: Yes, we have a white van, 2 or 3 guys in there, they look like Palestinians and going around a building.
Caller: There's a minivan heading toward the Holland tunnel, I see the guy by Newark Airport mixing some junk and he has those sheikh uniform.

---

[17] Confidential sources, Jersey City Police Department.

Dispatcher: He has what?
Caller: He's dressed like an Arab.[18]

It is clear that the Jersey City Police Department's emergency 911 call tapes were manipulated to delete any calls that might implicate the Israelis. The one call provided to WNBC was clearly an attempt at a "false flag" operation implicating "Palestinians" wearing "sheik uniforms" as the culprits in at least one of the white vans driven by Israeli "movers" on the morning of September 11.

After the van was traced to the Israeli moving company, the BOLO went out for the arrest of the vehicle's driver and passengers. An East Rutherford policeman directing traffic away from the closed Lincoln Tunnel on Route 3 East noticed the van was driving slowly on the service road towards the tunnel. The tag of the vehicle was only off by one letter from what was contained in the BOLO (JRJ 13Y) and the front New Jersey plate had been removed. It is very possible that to confuse the police, the Israelis were using NJ plate JRJ 13Y as the rear tag on two white vans – the one sighted in Liberty State Park and the other in Maria's apartment building parking lot. In fact, local police reported a number of white van sightings during September 11, with a number of them phoned into the police. Maria told ABC News she phoned tag number JRJ 13Y to the Jersey City Police after seeing the Israelis driving in a white van celebrating the first plane's impact, while Liberty State Park witnesses said the

---

[18] "911 Tapes tell Horror of 9/11," WNBC-TV, June 17, 2002 <http://www.wnbc.com/news/1315651/detail.html>

same tag number -- JRJ 13Y -- had been passed to the police and FBI after a white van with "celebrating Arabs" had been chased from the park by the park's chief ranger after the first plane impact.[19] These Israelis would become generally called the "dancing Israelis." It was clear that officials of New Jersey's Department of Environmental Protection in Trenton, which has authority over the state's parks, ordered Liberty State Park officials not to talk to the media about September 11 and the Israeli van.[20]

The East Rutherford Police report on the Israeli van states:

"Officer assigned to Special Detail on Route 3 was rerouting traffic on Highway 3 East to Hwy 120 and 3 West. Lincoln Tunnel was shut down and officer was diverting traffic. Officer notified by dispatch of a National Broadcast to be on lookout for 2000 Chevy Van White, NJ tag JYJ 13Y. 3 to 4 occupants. Officer noticed van traveling at slow speed east towards Lincoln Tunnel on the Service Road with 2 occupants visible. Officer informed sergeant of possible match. No front license plate but JRJ 13Y tag may have one letter off from National Broadcast. Sergeant told officer to stop vehicle because van seen in Liberty State Park at time of first impact. Driver did not exit vehicle. He fumbled with a black "fanny pack." Officer removed driver and van was searched. County bomb squad and FBI notified. FBI Newark ordered occupants to be held for prints because occupants were seen in Liberty State Park at time of first impact. 5 individuals were detained. Vehicle registration and insurance card

_____

[19] Management and residents of Liberty State Park Marina and personnel of Liberty State Park Water Taxi.
[20] Repeated phone calls, October 2004, with Liberty State Park and Department of Environmental Protection officials.

were obtained. Officer spoke to FBI Special Agents Robert F. Taylor, Jr., Bill Lloyd, and Dave O'Brien. Prior to transportation to NJ State Police Barracks at Giants Stadium, driver said, "We are Israelis, we are not your problem. Your problems are our problem. Palestinians are the problem." [21]

After the Israelis were arrested they misrepresented their location to one of the arresting police officers, Scott DeCarlo, claiming they were driving on West Side Highway in Manhattan when the planes struck the Trade Center. Dogs provided by the Bergen County Police K-9 unit alerted to the presence of explosives in the van. The nearby Homestead Studio Suites Hotel was evacuated for several hours. Asked about the Israelis in the van being present at Liberty State Park at the time of the first World Trade Center impact, one East Rutherford officer responded, "sure they were there."[22] Another confidential source told the *Bergen County Record*, "There are maps of the city in the car with certain places highlighted . . . It looked like they're hooked in with this. It looked like they knew what was going to happen when they were at Liberty State Park."[23] According to several Weehawken neighbors of the Urban Moving Systems warehouse, the FBI, upon searching the warehouse, discovered fertilizer, other chemicals for making explosives, pipes, caps, and traces of anthrax. After anthrax was discovered,

[21] East Rutherford Police information.
[22] Ibid.
[23] Paulo Lima, "Five Men Detained as Suspected Conspirators," *The Record* (Bergen County), September 12, 2001.

investigators wearing hazardous material suits went through the warehouse. Residents around Urban Moving Systems who had connections to the local police also reported that helicopters with infrared radar swooped in over the warehouse on several occasions.[24]

According to the ABC 20/20 report and echoing the East Rutherford police report, the van's driver, Sivan Kurzburg, told DeCarlo, "We are Israeli. We are not your problem. Your problems are our problems. The Palestinians are the problem."[25] The Israelis also reportedly told police they were tourists.[26] When the FBI developed the photos taken by the Israelis of the World Trade Center carnage, one photo depicted Kurzburg flicking a cigarette lighter in a celebratory manner with the burning buildings in the background.[27]

---

[24] Interviews with residents of "The Shades," the Weehawken neighborhood where Urban Moving Systems was located.

[25] Miller, op. cit.

[26] Lima, op. cit.

[27] Doug Saunders, "U.S. arrests of Israelis a mystery Most charged with immigration violations either have been deported or will be," *Globe and Mail* (Toronto), December 17, 2001, p. A7.

The Liberty State Park vantage point the five Urban Moving Systems celebrants had of lower Manhattan on the morning of September 11.

On the morning of September 12, the FBI canvassed the residents of the Israelis' apartment building, The Doric, in Union City. They asked the residents if they could identify photographs of the five Israelis.[28] The three Newark-based FBI agents on the case were Robert F. Taylor, Jr., Bill Lloyd and Dave O'Brien, the same agents who questioned the van drivers arrested in East Rutherford. All have subsequently been transferred from the Newark Field Office. A Union City off-duty policemen, who saw three people at Union Park next to the Doric Temple at the corner of 9th Street and Palisades Avenue in Union City. The three, who matched the description of other Israeli "false flag" teams,

---

[28]Robert Rudolph, Kate Coscarelli, and Brian Donohue, "Evidence takes investigators through Wayne and Fort Lee," *Newark Star-Ledger*, September 15, 2001.

were filming New York City's skyline before the first plane hit the World Trade Center. The officer also witnessed the three high-fiving each other. The officer chased the celebrants on foot but was unable to apprehend them. The officer later reported the three headed into Jersey City by car.[29]

The Newark FBI Field Office's files would have contained pre-9/11 intelligence on what occurred on September 11, 2001. In October 2000, an Israeli veteran of the Israel Defense Force overheard a conversation between three men in the Gomel Chesed Cemetery in Newark, New Jersey. The three men speaking in Hebrew were discussing the "planes hitting the twins," a reference to the 9/11 attacks some 11 months later. The FBI Newark office was informed of the conversation. There was no follow-up by the FBI.

On 9/11, another suspicious van carrying explosives was stopped by police on an approach ramp to the George Washington Bridge from the New Jersey side. Police suspected the perpetrators were trying to blow up the bridge.[30]

According to Jersey City police sources, FBI agent Monica Patton investigated the activities of Israeli "movers" and four of the hijackers, Mohammed Atta, Marwan al Shehhi, and two Saudi brothers – Waleed M. and Wail Al-Shehri -- at the same video rental store in Jersey City. One of the videos the Saudi brothers rented was an HBO documentary on the 1993 bombing of the World Trade Center. Another video they

---

[29] Interviews of Union City and Weehawken witnesses to 911 attack, October 2004.
[30] "Car bomb found on George Washington Bridge," *Jerusalem Post*, September 12, 2001.

rented was "The Towering Inferno." The video storeowner said his video rental records were later stolen after the FBI interviewed him and he told them about the Saudis' rental history. The Al Shehri brothers also purchased phone cards from the video store for special use in calling Dubai. The Jersey City intrigue does not stop with the Saudis and Israelis. Jersey City Police also reported that the business card of a Jersey City municipal government social worker had been found on Timothy McVeigh after his arrest for the bombing of the Murrah Federal Building in Oklahoma City in 1995.[31]

After serving two and a half months in prison and after a barrage of official complaints from the Israeli government, the five Israeli "movers" (Kurzberg, his brother Paul Kurzberg, Yaron Shmuel, Oded Elner, and Omer Marmari) were released over the objections of the CIA and permitted to return home. However, when Jersey City police checked the Israelis' van they found $4,700 hidden in a sock, two foreign passports and a Stanley-knife box cutter (the same brand used by the 9/11 hijackers). Paul Kurzberg, refused for ten weeks to take a polygraph and then flunked it when he did. His lawyer said his client once worked for Israeli intelligence in "another country."[32] Jerusalem Mayor Ehud Olmert interceded twice with his good friend New York Mayor Rudolph Giuliani to have the Israelis released. On September 14, 2004, the five "dancing Israelis" filed suit against the United

---

[31] Interviews in Jersey City, October 2004.
[32] Miller, op. cit.

States in U.S. District Court in Brooklyn for wrongful arrest and imprisonment.

In their complaint, Silvan Kurzberg, Paul Kurzberg, Yaron Shmuel, Omer Gavriel Marmari, and Oded Oz Elner cited the following defendants:

JOHN ASHCROFT, Attorney General of the United States; JAMES W. ZIGLAR (Former Commissioner of the Immigration and Naturalization Service); MICHAEL ZENK (Warden of the Metropolitan Detention Center); DENNIS HASTY (former Warden of the Metropolitan Detention Center) KATHLEEN HAWK SAWYER (former Director of the Federal Bureau of Prisons); LINDA THOMAS (former Associate Warden of Programs of the Metropolitan Detention Center); ROBERT MUELLER (Director of the Federal Bureau of Investigation); KEVIN LOPEZ (believed to be an employee of the Federal Bureau of Prisons); S. CHASE (believed to be an employee of the Federal Bureau of Prisons); "JORDAN" (believed to be an employee of the Federal Bureau of Prisons, whose true first and last names are unknown to the plaintiffs, who believe they heard him being called "Jordan") MARIO MACHADO (believed to be an employee of the Federal Bureau of Prisons); WILLIAM BECK (believed to be an employee of the Federal Bureau of Prisons); RICHARD DIAZ (believed to be an employee of the Federal Bureau of Prisons); C. SHACKS (first name unknown first name unknown, believed to be an employee of the Federal Bureau of Prisons); SALVATORE LOPRESTI (believed to be an employee of the Federal Bureau of Prisons); STEVEN BARRERE (believed to be an employee of the Federal Bureau of Prisons); JON OSTEEN (believed to be an employee of the Federal Bureau of Prisons); J. MIELES (first name unknown, believed to be an employee of the Federal Bureau of Prisons); MICHAEL DEFRANCISCO (believed to be

*an employee of the Federal Bureau of Prisons); F.
JOHNSON (first name unknown, believed to be an
employee of the Federal Bureau of Prisons);
CHRISTPHOR WITSCHEL (believed to be an
employee of the Federal Bureau of Prisons);
MOSCHELLO (first name unknown, believed to be an
employee of the Federal Bureau of Prisons); NORMAN
(first name unknown, believed to be an employee of the
Federal Bureau of Prisons); HOSAIN (first name
unknown, believed to be an employee of the Federal
Bureau of Prisons); MOUNBO (first name unknown,
believed to be an employee of the Federal Bureau of
Prisons); M. ROBINSON (first name unknown,
believed to be an employee of the Federal Bureau of
Prisons); TORRES (first name unknown, believed to be
an employee of the Federal Bureau of Prisons)
COUNSELOR RAYMOND COTTON (believed to be
an employee of the Federal Bureau of Prisons); DR.
LORENZO (first name unknown, believed to be an
employee of the Federal Bureau of Prisons);
LIEUTENANT BIRAR (first name unknown, believed to
be an employee of the Federal Bureau of Prisons);
LIEUTENANT BUCK (first name unknown, believed to
be an employee of the Federal Bureau of Prisons);
LIEUTENANT T. CUSH (first name unknown, believed
to be an employee of the Federal Bureau of Prisons);
LIEUTENANT GUSS (first name unknown, believed to
be an employee of the Federal Bureau of Prisons);
LIEUTENANT D. ORTIZ (first name unknown,
believed to be an employee of the Federal Bureau of
Prisons); LIEUTENANT J. PEREZ (first name
unknown, believed to be an employee of the Federal
Bureau of Prisons); UNIT MANAGER C. SHACKS
(first name unknown, believed to be an employee of the
Federal Bureau of Prisons); JOHN DOES 1-30,
Metropolitan Detention Center Corrections Officers,
"John Doe" being fictional first and last names,
intended to be the corrections officers at the
Metropolitan Detention Center who abused the*

*plaintiffs and violated their rights, and whose identities
are known to the defendants but at this time unknown
to the plaintiffs; JOHN ROES 1-30, Federal Bureau of
Investigation and/or Immigration and Naturalization
Service Agents, "John Roe" being
fictional first and last names, intended to be the
corrections officers at the Metropolitan Detention
Center who abused the plaintiffs and violated their
rights, and whose identities are known to the
defendants but at this time unknown to the plaintiffs.*

A number of interesting facts are stated in the
Israelis' complaint. It states that some of the
Israelis were classified as being "of high interest"
to the government's terrorism investigation,
"Witness Security" and/or "Management Interest
Group 155." They were "housed in one of the
most highly restrictive prison settings possible, the
Administrative Maximum Special Housing Unit
("ADMAX SHU") of the Metropolitan Detention
Center ("MDC")." The government was also
interested in the Israelis' possessions. The
complaint states the government "confiscated
personal identification, money, and valuable
personal items" from the Israelis. In addition, the
government searched the homes of the Israelis and
confiscated additional personal items.

One intriguing complaint was that the U.S.
government detained the Israelis precisely because
they were Jewish Israelis. The court filing states:
"Defendants and others have also engaged in
racial, religious, ethnic, and/or national origin
profiling. Plaintiffs' race, religion, ethnicity,
and/or national origin played a determinative role
in Defendants' decision to detain them initially, to
subject them to a blanket non-bond policy, to

subject them to punishing and dangerous conditions of confinement, and then to keep them detained beyond the point at which removal or voluntary departure could have been effectuated . . ."

Silvan Kurzberg was required to provide a blood sample while in prison, an indication that federal authorities may have had some DNA evidence they wanted to match. At the time of their arrest, all the Israelis had plane tickets back to Israel. When they were first detained, the Israelis were not permitted to meet with a rabbi. Later access to a rabbi was granted under "severely limited" circumstances. Prayer books and a bible given to the Israelis by the rabbi was inspected by prison guards. During their first two weeks of detention, the FBI prohibited the Israeli Counsel in New York from meeting with Israelis.

One of the most astounding claims of the Israelis was that the FBI, Bureau of Prisons, and Immigration and Naturalization Service did not understand the difference between Arab Muslims and Jewish Israelis. The complaint states: "The plaintiffs are Jewish Israelis, not Moslems, but due to the similarity of language and the geographical location of Israel in the Middle East, and the ignorance or lack of understanding of the Arab-Israeli conflict and the fact that Israel is an ally of the United States, the defendants mentally placed the plaintiffs in the same category as Moslems, and discriminated against them the same way."[33]

---

[33] First Amended Complaint, filed September 14, 2004 U.S. District Court, Eastern District of New York, 04 Civ. 3950 (JG) (CP).

At around noon on September 12, 2001, Roy
Barak, a former Israeli paratrooper, and Motti
Butbul, both employed by Urban Moving Systems
as drivers, were stopped by police near York,
Pennsylvania. They were en route from Chicago to
New York City. Police discovered Barak had an
expired visa and Butbul had no work permit. FBI
agents were soon on the scene and grew
suspicious when a box cutter was found inside the
truck. The FBI polygraphed Barak and showed
him a picture of his five colleagues arrested in
New Jersey and asked him why they were smiling.
Barak responded that they were not smiling. The
FBI thought Barak was a possible terrorist and a
Mossad spy. The FBI was particularly interested if
someone sent Barak to the United States and if, at
the time, he held a security clearance in the Israeli
army. Barak spent his second week in solitary
confinement without a television, radio, or any
books.[34]

Vince Cannistraro, the former operations
chief for counter-terrorism for the CIA, said that a
search of the CIA's national intelligence database
turned up some of the names of Israelis arrested in
New Jersey. He said a number of people in the
U.S. intelligence community concluded that Urban
Moving was a Mossad operation and the Israelis
were pursuing Islamist radicals in the New Jersey-
New York area and particularly in Patterson, New
Jersey. Pauline Stepkovich, who lived across the
street from Urban Moving, told ABC News that
FBI agents removed about a dozen boxes and

---

[34] Galloway, op. cit.

computers, enough to fill up two SUVs. Cannistraro told ABC News that the FBI was concerned that the Israeli movers had some advanced knowledge of the 9/11 attacks but failed to warn the United States. "The fear of some of the FBI investigators in this particular case was that this group had some advanced knowledge of what was going to happen on 9/11. And once they understood there was an Israeli connection--an Israeli intelligence connection--they became very disturbed, because the implication was that the Israelis may have had some advanced knowledge of the events of 9/11 and hadn't told us," Cannistraro said.[35] Israeli intelligence foreknowledge about the 9/11 attacks was confirmed by two senior-level intelligence officials at the CIA and FBI.[36]

In Washington, Israeli embassy spokesman, Mark Regev, dismissed the espionage charges, claiming the excitement of the Israelis seeing the World Trade Center collapse was due to "youthful foolishness."[37] A lawyer for one of the Israelis said his client denied celebrating the terrorist attack on the Trade Center, however, after the FBI developed their film it clearly showed three of the Israelis on top of the van "smiling and clowning around" with the buildings burning in the background.[38] The evidence bolstered what Maria and Pat told the police and proved that the Israelis lied to the police when they claimed they were in Manhattan during the attack.

---

[35] John Miller, op. cit.
[36] Confidential information.
[37] Miller, op. cit.
[38] John Miller, op. cit.

The Jewish weekly newspaper, *The Forward*, reported that a top U.S. government official told it, "The assessment was that Urban Moving Systems was a front for the Mossad and operatives employed by it... the conclusion of the FBI was that they were spying on local Arabs."[39] ABC 20/20 host Barbara Walters commented on how the story of the Israeli movers was received in the Arab world, "The story is that Israel knew more than it would like to admit about the terrorist attack in this country. It's a rumor, but in some Arab countries--including Saudi Arabia, which I visited earlier this year--even educated people told me that they believe it is absolutely true."[40]

Perhaps the young Israelis were only mirroring the feelings of former Israeli Prime Minister Benjamin Netanyahu, who when asked how the 911 attacks would affect U.S.-Israeli relations, said, "It's very good... Well, it's not good, but it will generate immediate sympathy for Israel from Americans." Bergen County Police Chief John Schmidig was not as serene. He said, "We got an alert to be on the lookout for a white Chevrolet van with New Jersey registration and writing on the side. Three individuals were seen celebrating in Liberty State Park after the impact. They said three people were jumping up and down."[41]

***

---

[39] Marc Perelman, "Spy Rumors Fly on Gusts of Truth; Americans Probing Reports of Israeli Espionage," *The Forward*, March 15, 2002.
[40] John Miller, op. cit.
[41] Mackay, op. cit.

New Jersey has always been a hotbed for Mossad and Israeli organized crime activity, which are often indistinguishable from one another.

In 2009, the FBI rolled up a Syrian Jewish criminal syndicate that was involved in buying off local elected and appointed government officials in north Jersey is but one in a long series of law enforcement operations directed, sometimes unsuccessfully due to the immense power of the Israel Lobby in the United States, against Jewish criminal networks in the New Jersey-New York region. These criminal networks also have one important thing in common: close connections to Israeli politicians and businessmen.

The FBI used a confidential witness to identify a number of Syrian Jewish rabbis who were using synagogues and yeshivas as money laundering fronts reportedly for the illegal sale of knock-off designer hand bags and even human organs. The witness, Solomon Dwek, was a major real estate developer and gambling boat owner who was arrested in 2006 for trying to pass a bad check and defraud PNC Bank of $25 million. Dwek was a member of the powerful Syrian Jewish clan in New Jersey and New York, which has been called the "SY Empire" and the "Dwek clan."

Dwek's father, Isaac Dwek, served as a rabbi of a synagogue and yeshiva school in the Syrian Jewish enclave of Deal, New Jersey, on the Jersey shore. Deal is a nexus for the radical Israeli right that is opposed to any peace agreement with the Palestinians and the ultra-orthodox Israeli Shas Party, a member of the current Israeli coalition government, has held fundraisers in Deal. The

Syrian Jewish community is also heavily involved in worldwide Chabad Houses, which WMR has previously linked to drug smuggling and money laundering, particularly in Mumbai, Bangkok, and other Asian cities. In 1992, the Syrian government lifted travel restrictions and limits on the disposition of property for the Syrian Jewish community. Syrian Jews were relatively free to travel, including to the United States.

Among the rabbis arrested was Saul Kassin, the 87-year-old chief rabbi of the 80,000-member Syrian Jewish community in Brooklyn and New Jersey. Rabbis from Brooklyn and Deal were also arrested for money laundering operations that used the tax-exempt status of Jewish religious organizations to avoid detection and reporting to the government.

The mayors of Hoboken, Secaucus, and Ridgefield were also arrested as part of the bribery probe of the Syrian Jewish syndicate, as well as a Jersey City state assemblyman and an Ocean Township mayor and assemblyman. A member of New Jersey Governor Jon Corzine's cabinet was also arrested, along with appointed officials in Bayonne, Hoboken, and Jersey City.

The latest reported criminal activity among the region's Syrian Jewish community is nothing new. One prominent member of the community, which traces its origins back to the Syrian city of Aleppo, was Eddie Antar, the owner of a regional chain of consumer electronics stories called "Crazy Eddie's," fled the United States for Israel after being indicted for fraud.

Antar had laundered some $80 million through Panamanian and Israeli banks, much of it ending up at the Bank Leumi in Tel Aviv, Swiss banks, a "folding tent" Liberian company, and a Liechtenstein foundation. Antar used a fake passport and the alias of David Jacob Levi Cohen to enter Israel. Antar also used the alias of Alexander Stewart. Antar was eventually arrested near Tel Aviv and was extradited back to the United States where he eventually received an eight-year prison sentence. The chief federal prosecutor against Antar was Michael Chertoff.

Syrian-Jewish businessman Norman Jemal, the head of another influential Syrian-Jewish family and a consumer electronics competitor of Crazy Eddie, saw his store chain Nobody Beats the Wiz, collapse into bankruptcy in 2003.

Another prominent Syrian Jew was Edmond Safra who founded Banco Safra in Brazil in 1955. The Beirut-based Safra family had long served as important bankers for the Ottoman Empire. Safra eventually became a billionaire banking and investment tycoon. Safra founded the Republic National Bank in New York in 1966. In 1999, Safra was killed in an arson attack on his Monte Carlo home. Safra's U.S.-born nurse, Ted Maher, who described himself as a former U.S. Army Green Beret, was arrested and charged with starting the fire, convicted and released after serving a prison sentence. Safra's killer or killers still remain at large. Safra's security chief, Shmuile Cohen, had recruited a number of Israeli military Special Forces personnel to guard Safra, but Shmule and the guards were given the night off by Safra's wife. Before his death, Safra was negotiating the sale of Republic Bank to HSBC. Safra was also cooperating with the FBI in its probe of the use of U.S. banks by the Russian-Israeli mafia to launder billions of dollars. There is speculation that Safra was murdered by the Russian-Israeli mob to keep him from divulging more details of their operations to the FBI.

After the recent bust of prominent Syrian-Jews in New Jersey and New York, the FBI and Justice Department revealed their investigation had lasted for ten years. The Safra murder occurred ten years prior to the recent corruption arrests. WMR has learned that the FBI is actually probing a much bigger criminal syndicate, one that involves more powerful politicians and businessmen involved in real estate and financial services in New York and New Jersey.

One prominent member of the Syrian Jewish community is Joseph Cayre, the real estate business partner of Larry Silverstein and Lloyd Goldman in the pre-9/11 lease of the World Trade Center from the New York-New Jersey Port Authority and the subsequent re-development of the "Ground Zero" site. Silverstein, Cayre, Goldman, and New York Mayor Michael Bloomberg have recently been feuding with the Port Authority over the terms of the re-development scheme. Part of the re-development strategy is central to the "Cornerstones Project," a project to establish for mega-entertainment and sports complexes in Manhattan connected to two other such centers on Coney Island and at the Meadowlands Xanadu entertainment and shopping complex in East Rutherford, New Jersey, next to Secaucus. The Xanadu project is being underwritten by Goldman Sachs and was a favorite of Governor Jon Corzine, a former chairman of Goldman Sachs.

In the criminal complaint against Rabbi Eliahu "Eli" Ben Haim of the Ohel Yaacob

58

congregation in Deal, a co-conspirator only identified as "I.M.," who is based in Israel and was a principal source of cash for Ben Haim, is cited. It was odd that "I.M." was only identified by initials when two other co-conspirators of Ben Haim were identified by their full names: Schmulik Cohen of Brooklyn and Arye Weiss, also of Brooklyn. "I.M.'s" modus operandi was described in the criminal complaint:

"Defendant BEN HAIM also mentioned that he owed another individual $495,000. This individual, according to defendant BEN HAIM, had wired money from Hong Kong to Israel, and stated that 'he has money in Hong Kong from his –- the kickbacks from the factories.' Defendant BEN HAIM also further described the activities of Coconspirator I.M. in the following terms: 'the head contact's in Israel . . . He has different people, he has, . . . he has a hundred cus-, no customer in New York [u/i] [unintelligible] money in Israel [u/i] real estate investments, they, they want to hide their money. They don't want it to show. So they give the cash here to him and he gives me the cash . . . You see the merry-go-round? This guy's been doing it for 20, 30 years.' Defendant BEN HAIM also indicated that he would pick up cash, as coordinated by Coconspirator I.M., at locations in Brooklyn. The CW [confidential witness] offered to pick up the cash that defendant BEN HAIM anticipated would be available to him the following week."

The complaint provided even greater details of "I.M.'s" money laundering activities:

"Defendant BEN HAIM told the CW about 'customers from two, three years ago that are calling me,' and indicated that "[t]hat's a signal that the market is tight.' Defendant BEN HAIM also discussed his source for cash, Coconspirator I.M., and stated that he spoke to Coconspirator I.M. '[e]very day - every other day.' Referring to Coconspirator I.M., defendant BEN HAIM then asked the CW '[d]id you know that he had me in the last 4 years send out wires every time to a different place in the world to a different name? It's unbelievable. I never saw anything like it.' When the CW asked whether defendant BEN HAIM was referring to different locations in only Israel, defendant BEN HAIM replied '[n]o, all over the world. . . All over the world. From Australia to New Zealand to Uganda. I mean [u/i] every country imaginable. Turkey, you can't believe it. . . . All different names. It's never the same name. . . . Switzerland, everywhere, France, everywhere, Spain . . . . China, Japan.' Defendant BEN HAIM also explained that the market for cash was tight 'only in the beginning of the year and the end of the year.'"

It appears that the FBI was being careful about naming "I.M." due to his extensive contacts from Israel to countries around the world, an indication that "I.M.," unlike the rabbis and the New Jersey politicos, was a big fry who was laundering large sums of money, possibly from gambling operations, through synagogues and Jewish charities. It was known that Solomon Dwek was involved in a casino boat business and that jailed GOP lobbyist Jack Abramoff was similarly involved in taking control of Sun Cruz Casino boats in Florida. Abramoff also funded radical

60

Israeli settler movements on the West Bank. The identity of "I.M,", if ever revealed, would have served as a body blow to the Likud government of Netanyahu and his major coalition partners, Yisrael Beiteinu of extreme right-wing Foreign Minister Avigdor Lieberman and the ultra-orthodox Shas Party. The revelation of "I.M.'s" identity, the author was told, would provide encouragement to the Palestinians to stand their ground against Israeli encroachment in east Jerusalem and the West Bank. In fact, the timing of the arrests of the Syrian Jews in New Jersey and New York may have been directly tied to Israel's move to build a residential complex in east Jerusalem over the objections of President Barack Obama.

On July 26, 2009, the Israeli newspaper *Yedioth Ahronoth* reported that Rabbi David Yosef, the son of Shas spiritual leader and former Chief Rabbi of Israel Rabbi Ovadia Yosef, left the Long Branch, New Jersey home of Ben-Haim for Israel just hours before the FBI raid that saw the arrest of Ben-Haim. In May, Aryeh Deri visited the Syrian-Jewish community in the New York-New Jersey region seeking funds for a new political party. Deri's successor as the head of Shas, Eliyahu "Eli" Yishai, served as Interior Minister and a Deputy Prime Minister of Israel.

Ovadia Yosef condemned President Barack Obama for pressuring Israel on the freeze of settlements. Yosef also called for the rebuilding of the Jewish temple on the site of the Al Aqsa mosque in Jerusalem, one of Islam's holiest sites. Yosef complained that there "are Arabs there."[42]

---

[42] July 27, 2009, "North Jersey: epicenter of "Kosher

There were other connections between Israeli criminal elements and terrorist attacks in the United States:

- ➢ A Syrian Jew named Rimon Alkatri was indicted by a New York City grand jury for phoning a false terrorist threat to the New York City police in May 2006. The indictment charged Alkatri with making a false terrorist threat in the first degree. Alkatri was arrested on July 31, 2006, a little over a week from the hype generated by the "great airplane liquid bombing hoax." Alkatri, who owns the El Castillo de Oro jewelry store on Knickerbocker Avenue in Brooklyn and who arrived in the United States in 1996, was arrested by police while he was leaving his apartment in a Syrian Jewish neighborhood on East 9th Street. In May, Alkatri, using the alias Jose Rodriguez, and claiming to be from Israel, said he overheard five Syrian employees of his store use the phrase "Allahu Akbar" (God is great) and that they were plotting to hide explosives in hollowed-out jewelry and perpetrate a suicide bombing in the New York subway system on the Fourth of July. Police later discovered that the five Syrian "conspirators" identified by Alkatri were not even Muslims, but Christians and Jews. Alkatri, who could have been sentenced to seven years in jail, was given a six month sentence.

Nostra" and Mossad activity," WayneMadsenReport.com

➢ In 2003, Yehuda Abraham, a dual U.S.-Israeli citizen, global diamond dealer and native of Afghanistan, was charged with money laundering for an Indian weapons smuggler named Hemant Lakhani who was attempting to purchase Russian portable missile launchers to bring down American passenger planes, including Air Force One, in the United States. Abraham was later convicted in the scheme that also involved a Malaysian bag man associated with the Southeast Asian Al Qaeda off-shoot Jemaah Islamiya. Abraham and Lakhani conducted their meetings near Newark International Airport. Abraham was sentenced to home detention.

**

A Federal Aviation Administration (FAA) source told the author that in the months before 9/11, an Israeli-run car wash opened two blocks north of the FAA's regional office in Atlanta. A young Israeli man ran the car wash. The man lived with an older man who claimed to be his uncle. The Israelis were very interested in striking up social relationships with FAA employees who used the car wash.

In the days before the 9/11 attacks, the Israelis at the car wash disappeared suddenly.

In Israel and the Los Angeles and New York City areas, Israeli car washes have been associated by law enforcement with criminal underworld activities. In January 2004, two Israeli nationals, Israel Or and Yossi Ben-Sadon, robbed at gunpoint more than $150,000 from an Upper

East Side car wash in Manhattan and subsequently fled to Israel.

Car washes have also featured prominently in past Israeli espionage cases. The notorious convicted Israeli spy Jonathan Pollard used Sam's Car Wash in Suitland, Maryland to pass suitcases full of highly-classified documents to his Israeli embassy Mossad handler every Friday for eighteen months. In Riverdale, in The Bronx, a hotbed of Jewish agitation groups seeking to release Pollard from federal prison, resides a suspected Mossad officer who once lived next door to Pollard. The man also happened to work at a car wash.[43]

---

[43] September 17-19, 201, "Add car washes to the Mossad fronts in the United States," WayneMadsenReport.com

Chapter 4 -- Pushback by Israel against the Media

It is no coincidence that both Fox News and KHOU-TV had to pull down their web stories on the Israeli art students (based on the exposés in *Intelligence Online* and *Le Monde*, Fox began referring to its original December 2001 story on its web site). According to a number of Washington journalists, any time an article critical of Israel appears in the U.S. press, reporters and editors can expect to hear from a Boston-based group called the Committee for Accuracy in Middle East Reporting in America or "CAMERA." The Kafkaesque group makes no secret of its aggressive intimidation methods. Its web site states: "CAMERA systematically monitors, documents, reviews and archives Middle East coverage. Staffers directly contact journalists and publishers concerning distorted or inaccurate coverage… CAMERA members are encouraged to write letters both to the publication or network, and to the sponsors or advertisers… If corrections and improved coverage are not forthcoming, we publicize the faulty reporting and the journalist's refusal to admit error."

As an example, CAMERA cited a *Washington Post* story that refuted the legitimacy of the DEA's investigation and report on the Israeli art students. The story by reporters John Mintz and Dan Eggen questioned the motive behind the DEA's report by claiming, without offering any proof, that the agent who wrote it was disgruntled. Moreover, there was more than one author of the report. Apparently, CAMERA's "fact checkers" were only interested in checking out stories with which they disagreed or found embarrassing.

Neither the *Washington Post* nor CAMERA seemed all that much interested in a warning about the Israeli "art students" and their "aggressive" visits to the offices and homes of U.S. federal agents that was circulated in March, 2001 by the White House Office of the National Counterintelligence Executive. The warning stated:

> "In the past six weeks, employees in federal office buildings located throughout the United States have reported suspicious activities connected with individuals representing themselves as foreign students selling or delivering artwork. Employees have observed both males and females attempting to bypass facility security and enter federal buildings.
>
> If challenged, the individuals state that they are delivering artwork from a studio in Miami, Florida, called Universal Art, Inc., or that they are art students and are looking for opinions regarding their work. These individuals have been described as aggressive. They attempt to engage employees in conversation rather than giving a sales pitch.
>
> Federal police officers have arrested two of these individuals for trespassing and discovered that the suspects possessed counterfeit work visas and green cards. These individuals have also gone to the private

residences of senior federal officials under the guise of selling art."[44]

The nature of reporting on Israeli espionage in the United States can result in sources drying up rapidly. In the case of the DEA, the spokesman who originally confirmed the veracity and validity of the DEA Report was suddenly sent away on "vacation." Other DEA agents and employees of other Justice Department agencies began to seal their lips. Attorney General John Ashcroft refused on two occasions to comment on the DEA investigation. Congress was also unwilling to look into the matter. Asked why, a senior congressional staffer replied, "You've got to be kidding... This is an election year!" He was referring to the 2002 congressional elections.

Ashcroft was portrayed as "disinterested" in counterterrorism during the summer of 2001, according to internal FBI memos written by Acting Director of the FBI Thomas Pickard.[45] Ashcroft's "disinterest" in terrorism did not affect his looking out for his own safety. At the end of July 2001, Ashcroft broke with precedence and flew in a private G-3 Gulfstream to go on a fishing trip to Missouri. Ashcroft had previously flown on commercial planes. When asked why Ashcroft did not fly commercial, the Justice Department said that because of a "threat assessment" by the FBI, Ashcroft would "travel only by private jet for the remainder of his term." Neither the FBI nor the Justice Department would identify what the threat

---

[44] <http://www.ncix.gov/news/2001/mar01.html#a1>
[45] Philip Shenon, "FBI and Ashcroft to Come under Fire," *International Herald Tribune*, April 6, 2004.

was, when it was detected or who made it. However, the FBI security detail for Ashcroft determined that the threat was critical enough for Ashcroft not to fly on commercial aircraft.[46]

The FBI ignored both the warnings about Israeli art students and Arab hijackers. The two groups' paths crossed in a number of U.S. cities in 2000.

After the DEA Report was leaked, I met with a journalist colleague who was also covering the art student story and had high level contacts within the Justice Department and FBI. During our meeting at the Navy Memorial just across the street from the National Archives, he summed up the problem: the cover-up went right to the top

---

[46] Jim Stewart, "Ashcroft Flying High," CBS News, July 26, 2001.

and the primary culprits were John Ashcroft and FBI Director Robert Mueller.

The Israelis were described in the DEA Report and other security advisories as being part of an "organized intelligence gathering activity." According to the FBI list, the Arab terrorist and suspect cells lived in the same neighborhoods as the Israeli cells in Irving, Texas and Hollywood and Miami, Florida from Dec. 2000 to April 2001. In the case of Irving, the Israeli cell used a rental mailbox in a shopping center just one block away from an Arab suspect's apartment. In Hollywood, the terrorists, including lead hijacker Mohammad Atta, the Egyptian who piloted American Airlines Flight 11 into the North Tower of the World Trade Center, used a rental mailbox drop two blocks from an apartment rented by an Israeli "art student" team leader.

If the Israelis were stalking the hijackers, they would have also likely known about their interest in the World Trade Center. Speaking at a press conference in Washington, DC on March 22, 2004, William Rodriguez, the President of the Hispanic Victims Group and a 20-year veteran employee of the World Trade Center, revealed that he spotted Mohand Al-Shehri (alias Mohammed al Shehhi), one of the terrorist hijackers of United Flight 175 that crashed into the South Tower of the World Trade Center, two and a half months before September 11. Rodriguez said he saw Al-Shehri, a Saudi citizen, casing the North Tower of the World Trade Center. Rodriguez's comments were part of the press conference partly organized by family members of 9/11 victims. The family members were calling for a full accounting by members of both the Clinton and Bush administrations about what they knew about the Al Qaeda threat to hijack planes prior to 9/11.

Rodriguez was a building manager for the World Trade Center and he held the master key for the North Tower. He was the last survivor pulled by rescue workers from the rubble of the building after it collapsed.

Rodriguez said Al-Shehri asked him how many public bathrooms were in the building and, in retrospect, Rodriguez believed the terrorist was looking for ways to place additional explosives in the building prior to the airplane attack. Rodriguez also said as he was climbing the stairs to help rescue people after American Airlines Flight 11 struck his building he heard heavy equipment being moved around on the 34th floor, which was closed and locked for renovation. In the chaos, Rodriguez did not have time to open the doors to the 34th floor to find out who was there but he believed there might have been additional explosives placed inside the building. Rodriguez also claimed that while assisting evacuees he heard non-aircraft-related explosions coming from floors below his location on the 33rd floor. The former chief economist for the Bush Labor Department, Morgan Reynolds, believed the Bush administration's story about the World Trade Center collapse was "bogus." Reynolds, who was the director of the Criminal Justice Center at the National Center for Policy Analysis in Dallas and later professor emeritus at Texas A&M University, opined that "if demolition destroyed three steel skyscrapers [the Twin Towers and Building 7] at the World Trade Center on 9/11, then the case for an 'inside job' and a government attack on America would be compelling."

Reynolds added, "The government's collapse theory is highly vulnerable on its own terms. Only professional demolition appears to account for the full range of facts associated with the collapse of the three buildings."[47]

Moreover, Rodriguez passed along several of his tips about pre-9/11 surveillance of the World Trade Center to the FBI but he said the agency never bothered to talk to him. However, according to the August 6, 2001 President's Daily Brief, the FBI was aware that suspected terrorists were conducting surveillance of buildings in New York. The White House revealed that prior to 9/11, the FBI interviewed two Yemenis it detained for taking photographs of buildings in Federal Plaza in New York City. The FBI released them after determining the Yemenis were "tourists."[48] Yemen is the birthplace of Osama bin Laden and a number of Al Qaeda operatives hail from Yemen.

Of course, not everyone within the FBI was asleep at the wheel. Minneapolis Special Agent Coleen Rowley tried in vain to get a wiretap on Zacarias Moussaoui. Phoenix Special Agent Kenneth J. Williams reported flight training by Arab students connected to Bin Laden. John P. O'Neill, the FBI's top counterterrorism agent, constantly raised the problem of Saudi support for Al Qaeda, only to be rebuffed, and eventually, hounded out of the bureau by his superiors.

[47] John Daly, "UPI Hears," June 13, 2005 < http://washingtontimes.com/upi-breaking/20050613-102755-6408r.htm?
[48] Edward Alden, "White House publicizes CIA briefing to Bush," *Financial Times*, April 11, 2004.

The internal DEA report from June 2001 dealt with attempts by teams of Israeli "art students" to penetrate the security of various Federal buildings and offices throughout the United States. The DEA refused to officially comment on the report but a high-level source within the agency reports that it was the product of a larger investigation conducted jointly by a DEA and Immigration and Naturalization Service (INS) Operational Task Force set up in 2000 specifically to investigate the Israelis.

A number of the art students, who claimed they were from either Bezalel University in Jerusalem or the University of Jerusalem, said they answered ads in Israeli newspapers but could not give details of the identities of their bosses when interviewed by Federal agents. A number of the male and female art students, who were mainly in their early to mid 20s, had recently served in Israeli military and intelligence service, according to the report. Their activities were concentrated during the February-March 2001 time frame. More important, there was no University of Jerusalem and Bezalel said it had no record of any of the students having ever been enrolled there.

The DEA compiled an extensive list of the Israeli art students as an appendix (Indexing Section) to its report [LNU means "last name unknown"]:

"INDEXING SECTION:
1. BLAIN, Gat NADDIS negative, occupation: Israeli art student, sold painting to DEA employee in Dallas, TX on 01/04/2001 (Identified in paragraph 22)
2. FREIDMAN, Shabar NADDIS - Negative driver's license (#6728447), ID (#033056433)

3. AVRAHAM, Gerzon Ofir NADDIS - Negative.
DOB (08/12177), Israel passport (#6315574), Israeli
Ministries of Transport ID (#034193615)
4. L.N.U., Shahar NADDIS - Negative
5. BARAM, Lior NADDIS - Negative. Florida driver's
license (#B650-520-76-047-0), 10733 Cleary Blvd.,
#206, Plantation, Florida, 33324-0000, (DOB
02/07/76), 5'9", dark eyes and black hair
6, COHEN, Hammutal NADDIS - Negative DOB
(01/29/62), Israeli passport (#6077838), Immigration
departure (#41060016307 02/12/01), 5'8", 145 lbs.
7. RUBINSTEIN, Itay NADDIS - Negative DOB
(01/17/79), US, visa (#39127358), date of entry
12/23/00, Israeli passport (#39127358) *[sic, see visa]*,
6'0", 165 lbs.
8. AHARON, Ohad NADDIS - Negative
9. SEGAL, Yafit NADDIS - Negative
10. TOV, Yaniv Sheni NADDIS - Negative DOE
(06/02/74) NADDIS negative
11. DOR, Sahlev NADDIS - Negative DOB (08/08/77)
NADDIS negative
AJ
12. GROSS, Hagit NADDIS - Negative DOB
(09/30/78), Israeli passport (#5111696)
13. SHLOMO, Rony NADDIS - Negative
approximately 21 yoa
14. KOCHAVI, Inbar NADDIS - Negative Israeli
passport (#7674731)
15. DRORE, Rani NADDIS - Negative approximately
27 yoa
16. YOCHAI, Legurn NADDIS - Negative 13 753 SO
90th Ave., Mami, Florida 33176
17. MEYTAL, Cohen NADDIS - Negative. Address:
c/o Calmanovic, 3575 N. Beltline Rd,, P.0, Box 316,
Irving, Texas 75062. Addressed used by Michael
Calmanovic, identified below
18. SISSO, Rosie NADDIS - Negative.
19. BURKHOLDER, Seth Thomas NADDIS -
Negative. 3329 Bartlett Rd., Orlando, Florida, 1995

white Nissan pickup bearing Florida license plate D36-TTQ.

20. L.N.U., Elsa NADDIS - Negative.

21. SMITH, Travis Wayne NADDIS - Negative. white male, DOB (11/09/74), FBI No. 530083DBS (Assault - Domestic Violence) address: 615 S. Hardy, 4210, Tempe, Arizona

22. ESTRADA, Ramon Hispanic male, NADDIS - Negative. DOB (07/26/63), arrested 12/82 "processing marijuana for sale," 5/95 "transport/sell narcotics," 7/95 "transport/sell narcotics, adult giving minor narcotics, " 8/95 "domestic violence." FBI No. 7643 5FAG, CASID No. CA07401218, WASID No. WA17692473

23. GILOR, Yaniv Zacoravich NADDIS - Negative. registered owner of a 1997 Chevy van in San Diego, CA

24. MENDEL, Leviella NADDIS - Negative. 83 77 Tamar Drive, #37, Columbia, Maryland, DOB 10/29/75, Maryland driver's license #M-534-514-009-032, 5'7", 150 lbs. Additional inquiries revealed MENDEL has a new residential address, 4733 Haskell Ave., #46, Encino, California.

25. SILVER, Danny NADDIS - Negative. (NFI)
The Tampa, Florida District Office identified the following individuals (#26-942):

26. BENDALAK, Orit: NADDIS negative, DOB 10-28-78, WF, POB Israel, 5'7", 140 lbs., brown hair, brown eyes.

27. BEZALEL ACADEMY OF ARTS AND DESIGN: NADDIS negative, Jerusalem, 011-972-2-589-3333, www.bezalel.ac.il.

28. COHEN, Eli: NADDIS negative, 701 S. 21 Ave. #207, Hollywood, FL 33020, DOB 11/04/1977, FL DL C500-200-77-404-0, State of Israel Ministry of Transport card number 03379722

29. HARARI, Ilana: NADDIS negative, W/F, DOB 4-29-79, 9-29-79, 2-9-79, 14 Jerico Itolon Israel, attends

University of Jerusalem, 5'3", 90 lbs., brown hair, blue eyes, tattoo of sun on right foot.

30. KENDEL, Rachel: NADDIS negative, White/Female, State of Israel Ministry of Transport card number 7095201 and 034807727, Israeli passport number 6614254.

3 1, KUZNITZ, Keren: NADDIS - Negative. 1818 E. Oakland Park Blvd. #98, Fort Lauderdale, FL 33306, DOB 02/09/1979, 5'5"; FL driver's license: K253-500-79-549-0, State of Israel Ministry of Transport card number 7121535 and 035721844.

32. L.N.U, Nadav NADDIS - (NFI)

33. L.N.U., Tom NADDIS - Negative. White, male. Address: Hollywood/Ft. Lauderdale, Florida. Reportedly sells artwork to Israeli art students.

34. MARZIANO, Assaf or Asaf NADDIS negative, DOB 2-4-78, state of Israel Ministry of Transport # 034086959, passport #552306S, POB Israel, WM, 5'7", 150 lbs,

35. MATATIA, Keren: NADDIS negative (NFI)

36. OSHRA, Sussie: NADDIS negative. (NFI)

37. SASSOON, Sarah Minna: NADDIS negative, 2916 Pierce St., 94, Hollywood, FL 33020, DOB 11/8/1978, FL DL# S250-793-79-908-0.

38. SELLA, Livnet: NADDIS necgative, DOB 12/24/1978, State of Israel Ministry of Transport number 7023400 and 036208023, International Student Idenity card number S972-204-776-601.

39. SERFATY, Hanan, aka Hanane SARFATI: NADDIS negative, 4220 Sheridan St., #303, Hollywood, FL 33.021, and 701 S. 21 Ave., Hollywood, FL, DOB 06/03/1977, 6', FL DL S613-320-77-203-0, registered owner of red mini-van FL tag # U71 DLD, phone number (954) 478-1006, cellular phone number (954) 478-0961.

40, SIMON, Michael: NADDIS negative, w/m, 11-23-78, Aliebenliezel 82, Jerusalem, telephone number 97226768256, Israeli passport no. 8660008, POB Jerusalem, 6'1", 180 lbs., black hair, brown eyes.

41. VAKSHI, Inbal: NADDIS negative aka Bella POLLCSON, State of Israel Miriistry of Transport License number 7098663 and 036444842, International Student Identity Card number S972-204-775-487, DOB 02/03/1979.

42. ZAGURI, Oshirt: NADDIS negative, 701 S. 21 Ave., 4205, Hollywood, FL 33020, DOB 07/11/1977, 5'6", FL DL #Z260-640-77-75 1 -0..

43. WEISFELNER, Odfd NADDIS - Negative. (NFI)

44. KEDEM, Guy. NADDIS -Negative. This female left a business card stating EAG-Guy Kedem, European Art Group, Oil Paintings; phone number (720) 581-7076; Fax number (303) 336-7006. The (720) number is unlisted and the (303) number is a fax number for Heritage Creek Apartments, 650 South Dahlia Circle, Denver, Colorado. (NFI)

The following individuals were identified by the Ft. Meyers, Florida Resident Office (#45-48):

45. MEIRAV, Zwaig, NADDIS - Negative. w/f, thin build, short long dark hair, DOB: 2/9/76, US VISA control # 20003205620012, Israeli passport 97831088

46. MACHBUBI, Hilda, NADDIS - Negative. w/f DOB: 5/4/79, US VISA control # 2000397210011, Israeli passport # 6530284, FL ID #M211-320-79-664-0

47. SIMKIN, Nimrod, NADDIS - Negative. w/m, over 6' tall, curly hair, DOB: 9/2/77, FL DL# S525-620-77-3220

48, KEREN, Inbal, NADDIS - Negative. w/f, DOB: 7/17/79, US VISA control # 20001710300009, Israeli passport # 6082073

The following individuals were identified by the Richmond, Virginia District Office (#49-54):

49. KEDEM, Eran, NADDIS - Negative. w/m, Israel, dob 10/15/75, 5'11", 160 lbs., 12990 SW 74th St., Pine Crest, FL, Israeli ID 4031820079, Israeli driver's license #651007

50. PERLAS, Limor NADDIS - Negative. (NFI)
51. ASE, Shiri NADDIS - Negative. (NFI).
52. KEMETCH, Omit, a.k.a. KIMCHY, Ornit, NADDIS - Negative. w/f, dob 02/04/74, passport 96814521
53. MER, Shmrt NADDIS - Negative. (NFI)
54. BOUZAGLO, Kobi, NADDIS - Negative. cellular telephone 1-888-321-6213 (NFI)

The following individuals were identified by the Montgomery, Alabama District Office:
55. VALANSI, Marcelo, NADDIS - Negative. dob 11/24/77, Argentina passport #26316660, 901 S.E. 1st Ave., #2, Gainesville, FL., 617 E. University Ave., Gainesville, FL., 1436 Washington Ave., Miami, FL., registered owner of 1984 GMC Custom Van, Florida tag T11YZX., Argentina DNI26316660 card 4190961, speaks English and Spanish, Tel # (352)378-1485 (Identified in Paragraph 6)
56. VALANSI, Roberto, NADDIS - Negative. father of Marcelo VALANSI. Salguero 2468, Apartment 15, Buenos Aires (NFI) (Identified in Paragraph 10)
57. VALANSI, Graziela, NADDIS - Negative. mother of Marcelo VALANSI, Salguero 2468, Apartment 15, Buenos Aires (NFI) (Identified in Paragraph 10)
58. SAGES, Ester, NADDIS - Negative. dob 9/30/77, Israeli passport 96470399, Attornet 161, New York City, NY., Hotel Carlton, New York City, NY (Identified in Paragraph 6)
59. SAGES, Elyahu NADDIS - Negative. (deceased), father of Ester SAGES, (NFI) (Identified in Paragraph 9)
60. SAGES, Marjalit, NADDIS - Negative. Mother of Ester SAGES (NFI) (Identified in Paragraph 8)
61. DARDIC, Vanina Erika, NADDIS - Negative. dob 3/5/78, Argentina passport #10581811, 901 S.E. 1st Ave., Gainesville, FL. . Argentina DN126473227 card #J8557, speaks English, Hebrew, and Spanish,

girlfriend of VALANSI, citizen of Argentina and Israel
(Identified in Paragraph 4)
62. DARDIC, Mario, NADDIS Negative. father of
Vanina DARDIC (NFI) (Identified in Paragraph 9)
63. COHEN, Judith (maiden name) NADDIS -
Negative. mother of Vanina DARDIC (NFI) (Identified
in Paragraph 9)
64. GAVISH, Yael NADDIS - Negative. W/F Brown
hair, Brown eyes, DOB: Oct 03, 1978. Citz: Israel
Passport Number: 5013766 issued 12-03-92, expires 3-
12-2002 US Visa number 20001818940002 Class B-
1/B-2 issued July 05, 2000 Expires June 28, 2010.
65. BALHAMS, Meirav NADDIS - Negative. W/F
Brown hair, Brown eyes, 5'03" DOB: 10-03-78 Citz:
Israel. New York ED Card 4 140-614-039. Address:
354 Paterson Plank Road #1, Jersey City, NJ 07650

The following individuals were identified by the
Orlando D.O. on May 3, 2001:
66. SEGALOVITZ, Peer - NADDIS Negative, White,
male, Nationality: Israeli, DOB: 03-16-1974, POB
Israel, Address: 8187 N. University Drive Apt. 4129,
Tamarac, FL, entered the U.S. on B-2 class visa on
January 17, 2001. Former officer in Israeli Special
Forces 605 Battalion. Israeli Military ED # 5087989.
Encountered May 3, 2001 at the Orlando D.O.
Occupation: Israeli Art Vendor/Student. (Identified in
Paragraph 96)
67. SEGALOVITZ, Dror - NADDIS - Negative.
White, Male, Brother of Peer Segalovitz. ADD:
Address 8187 N. University Drive, Apt. Nationality:
Israel. Identified in Paragraph 98)
68. SABGUNDJIAN, Kathy - NADDIS: Negative.
(626) 358-6453 (626) 256-1027
69. SAGIV, Akyuz Shmuel - NADDIS: Negative.
White, Male, Israeli Passport # 8710426; DOB: 09-27-
1976; POB: Maaloot, Israel; Entered US In New York;
PN: 954712-2126. Associate of Peer Segalovitz and
Dror Segalovitz. (Identified in paragraph #99).

The following were identified at the Volk Field ANG Base, Camp Douglas, Wisconsin:

70. WATERMANN, Tsvi NADDIS - Negative, AKA: Watermann, Zvi; white, male, DOB: June 7, 1979; Address: Pri Megadim 36 Mevaseret Zion, Isreal; Israeli Passport # 5728101 expiration date July 20, 2002; U.S. visa class B1/B2 expiration date March 20, 2011; Israeli Ministry of Transport driver's license, number 7046942.

71. KANTOR, Gal Kal NADDIS - Negative. white, male, DOB: Sep 08, 1975, Address: Kibbuts Eilon NO Western Galilee, Israel 22845; Israeli Passport 8261507 expiration date of Oct 20, 2004; U.S. B1/B2 visa, control number 19993358160012, expiration date of Nov 30, 2009.

The following were identifed at Tinker AFB, Oklahoma:

72. OHANA, Yaron NADDIS - Negative. DOB: 02-04-78; POB: Haifa, Israel; Passport Number: 8421721 U.S. Visa Number:42252049.

73. KALFON, Ronen NADDIS - Negative. DOB: 04-13-76; POB: Haifa, Israel Passport Number :8168262; U.S. Visa Number: 3 5966019.

74. COHEN, Zeev NADDIS - Negative. DOB: 03-26-78; POB: Haifa, Israel, Passport Number: 5524033: U.S. Visa Number: 33331965.

75. TOPAZ, Naor NADDIS - Negative DOB: 06-08-77; POB: Haif, Israel Passport Number: 8081705; U.S. Visa Number: 33306515.

The following were identified by the Euless, TX Police Department on January 2nd, 2001, (refer to page 10):

76. LIFSHITZ, Gilad, NADDIS - Negative. W/M, DOB'09/17/1978

77. YANAY, Betzalel, NADDIS - Negative. W/M, DOB 09/04/1978

78. BITON, MoriN Miryam, NADDIS - Negative.
W/F; DOB 07/14/1980
79. SASSON, Dana, NADDIS - Negative. W/F, DOB
08/10/1980
80. TOUYZ, Keren, NADDIS - Negative. W/F, DOB
08/20/1978
81. TZOR, Noam, NADDIS - Negative. previous
owner of 1GAHG39K5SF112662, a 1995 Chev/Spt
owned by Gilad LIFSHITZ of 7535 N. Beltline Rd,
APt 316, Irving, Texas 75062.
82. ROTEM, Sharon, NADDIS - Negative. described
as a white male, DOB 03 -12-77, Israeli passport
number 7948317, street address: 6023 Moshe Dayan,
Holon, Israel.
83. MAIMON, Maya, NADDIS - Negative.
Nationality: Israel. Israeli passport number as 5467894,
US B1/B2 visa, DOB 26Dec1978, Issue Date:
18Oct2000, Expiration Date: 15Oct2010.
84.BADIHI, Nofar, NADDIS - Negative. Nationality
Israel. Israeli passport number 5640993, DOB
21/03/1979 (sic), Place of Birth: Israel, date of issue:
05/12/1993, date of expiry (sic): 04/12/1995; US Visa
B I/B2, issue date: 05Jul 1996, Expiry Date:
02JUL2006.
85. MARABOTTO, Marco NADDIS - Negative.
Airline tickets were found reflecting the travel of Maya
MAIMON and Marco MARABOTTO from DFW
airport to Albuquerque, NM via Delta flight 2238 on
March 24, 2001. Each ticket also reflected Delta flight
1944 from Las Vegas to DFW on April 1, 2001.
86. FERNANDEZS, Marco, NADDIS - Negative a.k.a.
Marco Antonio FERNANDEZ De Castro Marabotto,
DOB 13Apr1977, passport number 99390039611,
Issuing State: Mexico; place of birth: Mexico, date of
issue: 16Jul1999, expiration date: l6Jul2000.
87. REGEV, Gadi, NADDIS - Negative described as
DOB: 17Dec1975, Nationality: Israel, passport number
5454338, visa type: B1/B2, issuing post: Tel Aviv,
issue date: 05Nov1998, expiration date: 04Nov2008

88. ARTZI, Eyal, NADDIS - Negative Texas DL
19554509, and an expiration date of 06-27-07. address:
10334 Sandra Lynn Dr., Dallas, TX 75228. DOB 05-
27-1977, commercial database shows that ARTZI is
the owner of a 1993 Plymouth Acclaim, Texas plate:
J75FYB, date registered 08/21/2000, expiration date:
07/31/2001
89, SUSI, David, NADDIS Negative DOB 01/09/1975,
boyfriend of Maya MAIMON

The following were identified by I&NS - Dallas:
90. ELDAD, Dahan, NADDIS - Negative. W/M
Israeli, add: Oak IEH Apts. 1913 Estrada Parkway,
#228, Irving, TX. Arrested by I&NS March 26 2001.
(Identified in paragraph 39)
91. AFRICANO-Leon, Elsa Beatriz, NADDIS -
Negative. W/F Nationality: Colombia Add: Oak Hill
Apts. 1913 Estrada Parkway, #228, Irving, TX.
Arrested by I&NS March 26, 2001. (Identified in
paragraph 39)
92. LIVNI, Eran, NADDIS - Negative. W/M Israeli
Add: Oak Hill Apts. 1913 Estrada Parkway, #228,
Irving, TX Arrested by I&NS March 26, 2001.
(Identified in paragraph 40)
93. OFEK, Aran, NADDIS - Negative. W/M Israeli,
ADD: Oak Hill Apts. 1913 Estrada Parkway, #259,
Irving, TX., father is 2-star general in Israeli Army.
Arrested by I&NS March 26, 200 1. (Identified in
paragraph 40)
94, GAL, Michal, NADDIS - Negative. W/F, Israeli,
DOB 08/10/1979, POB Afula, Israel, INS A 75-894-
941, ADD: Oak Hill Apts. 1913 Estrada Parkway,
4259, Irving, TX, Alt add.: 22 Palisade Terrace,
Edgewater, NJ 01020 Tel: (201)224-0797 Arrested by
I&NS March 26, 2001. (Identified in paragraph 40)
95. GAVRIEL, Noam, NADDIS - Negative.
Nationality: Israel (Identified in paraggraph 40)
96. KRITZMAN, Netta, NADDIS - Negative.
Nationality: US Citizen (Identified in paragraph 40)

97. BAER, Ophir, NADDIS - Negative. W/K DOB 11/11/1956, Nationality: Israel, employed by AMDOCS, Ltd., add: 7845 La Cabeza Drive, Dallas, TX 75248, former add: 1125 East Campbell Rd., Richardson, TX, Tel: (972) 392-0473 & (214) 576-5741, SSN: 627-70-0979- (Identified in paragraph 42)

98. AMDOCS, Limited., NADDIS - Negative. add: 1390 Timberlake Manor Parkway, Chesterfield, MO, Tel: (314) 821-3242 (Identified in paragraph 43)

99. DOTAN, Boaz, NADDIS - Negative. 23 Abba Hillel, St. Ranat Gan, Israel, TX president of AMDOCS, Ltd. (Identified in paragraph 43)

100. WHITMAN, Beverly A., NADDIS - Negative. SSN: 400-88-4097, Treasurer of AMDOCS, Ltd. (Identified in paragraph 43)

101. CHRISTOFFEL, Gregory, NADDIS - Negative. SSN: 389-52-850, Secretary of AMDOCS, Ltd. (Identified in paragraph 43)

102. MOSHE, Eran, NADDIS - Negative. Israeli, I&NS A 75-894-459, averted by I&N on 03/26/2001, occup. Israeli art student (Identified in paragrph 44)

103. VAINSHTEIN, Julia, NADDIS - Negative. W/F Israeli, DOB 11/12/1978, POB: Russia, arrived DFW on 03/27/2001, Assoc: Michael CALMANOVIC (Identified in paragraph 46)

104. BORENSTEIN, Dilka, NADDIS - Negative. Israeli, DOB 03/15/1979, POB: Israel, former Israeli Military Intelligence Officer, Assoc: Michael CALMANOVIC (Identified in paragraph 46)

105. NAVAR, Ofir, NADDIS - Negative. Israeli, DOB 09/02/1979, POB: Israel, former Israeli Military Demolition/Explosive ordnance specialist (Identified in paragraph 46)

106. CALMANOVIC, Michael, NADDIS - Negative. W/M, Israeli, DOB 09/06/1-975, POB: Israel, registered owner of TX: L44-CVD, add: 3575 N. Beltline Rd., Apt. 316, Irving, TX., alt. add: 312 Rochelle Rd., Irving, TX, alt. add: 1103 Hidden Ridge #3018, Irving, TX alt. Add: 1913 Estrada Parkway,

Irving, TX 75061, alt. add: 11012 Ventura Blvd., Studio City, CA 91604 Tel: (214)882-5196, alt, add: 319 S. 177 Place, 4201, Seattle, WA 98148 Tel: (206) 244-7705, Tel: (214) 882-5196 / (214) 837-3574 / (469)446-1248 (214) 837-5996 (214) 876-1235 (217) 837-2056 former Israeli electronic intercept officer. Arrested by I&NS on April 4th, 2001, Posted $50K bond, (Identified in paragraph 46)

107. SIMON, Itay, NADDIS - Negative. W/M, Israeli, DOB 02/27/1978, POB: Israel, former Israeli military, add: 1103 Hidden Ridge #3018, Irving, TX, alt add: California Associate of Michael Calmanovic. Arrested by I&NS April 4, 2001 for violation of status, posted $50,000 bond. (Identified in paragraph 50)

108. LNU, Gilad, NADDIS - Negative. Tel: (214) 882-5196 (214) 876-1235 (Identified in paragraph 50)

109. LNU, Roy, NADDIS - Negative. Tel: (214) 837-3574 (Identified in paragraph 50)[49]

110. LNU, Mosh, NADDIS - Negative. Tel: (469) 446-1248 (Identified in paragraph 50)

111. LNU, Gil, NADDIS - Negative. Tel: (214) 837-5996 (Identified in paragraph 50)

112. LNU, Gasaf, NADDIS - Negative. Tel: (217) 837-2056 (Identified in paragraph 50)

113. ENGEL, Yoni, NADDIS - Negative. W/K DOB 09/14/1979, POB: Israeli Citizen, Israel, former company commander in Israeli military, arrived DFW on 03/28/2001, arrested by I&NS, St. Louis, MO on April 4th, 2001 (Identified in paragraph 51)

114. DAGAI, Yotam, NADDIS - Negative. DOB 04/06/1978, POB: Israeli Citizen, Israel, arrested by I&NS, St. Louis, MO on April 4th, 2001, arrived DFW on 03/28/2001. (Identified in paragraph 51)

---

[49] A Roy Laniado surfaced as a team leader with regard to Israeli art students arrested in Canada in 2003. Roy Barak, a driver for Urban Moving Systems, was arrested on September 12, 2001 by police in Pennsylvania.

115. ALROEI, Or, W/M DOB 08/08/1978, POB: Israeli Citizen, Israel, visited DEA St. Louis on 04/04/2001, Had Tel: (214) 882-5196 in his possession, Associate of Michael CALMANOVIC & Gil LNU. (Identified in paragraph 51)
116. RABINOVITZ, Eli, NADDIS - Negative. W/M, DOB 03/27/1979, U.S. passport E3701329518, 5'6", 175 lbs., brown hair (Identified in paragraph 51)
17. ADESA Golden Gate, NADDIS - Negative. add: 6700 Stevenson Blvd., Fremont, CA, registered owner of CA: 3LVAO1P (Identified in paragraph 51)
118. SADAN, Ben, NADDIS - Negative, W/M Israeli, approx. 24 yoa, Tel: (214) 562-1110, driver of Israeli art students encountered April 4, 2001 in St. Louis, MO.
119. BEN DOR, Tomer, NADDIS - Negative. W/M Israeli, 'DOB 08/24/1975, occup: Computer software engineer, employer: NICE, former Israeli military officer for patriot missile defense (Identified in paragraph 55)
120. GLIKMAN, Marina, NADDIS - Negative. W/F Nationality: Israel, DOB 12/15/1972 (Identified in paragraph 53)
121. AKIVA, Ronen, associate of Marina GLIKMAN, occup: computer programm employer: RETALIX, former Israeli military officer (Identified in paragraph 55)
122. RETALIX, USA, NADDIS - Negative. add: 8081 Royal Ridge Parkway, Irving, TX, formerly known as Point of Sale, Limited. (Identified in paragraph 55).
123. DOR, Hillel, NADDIS - Negative. W/M Israeli, DOB 04/06/1971. Associate of Marina GLIKMAN (Identified in paragraph 55)
124. MILLER, Zeev, NADDIS - Negative. W/M Israeli, DOB 09/04/1971, occup: student/software engineer, employer: RETALIX Israel (Identified in paragraph 55).
125. SHAKED, Barry, NADDIS - Negative, CEO of RETALIX (Identified in paragraph 55).

On April 30, 2001, the Air Force issued a security alert from Tinker Air Force Base in Oklahoma City concerning a "possible intelligence collection effort being conducted by Israeli art students." DEA, INS, FBI, and Environmental Protection Agency (EPA) offices received similar alerts. The FBI office in New Orleans reportedly received a "Counter terrorism Advisory Report regarding suspicious activities around Federal buildings that related to Israeli students" in February 2000. The FBI also reported that an Israeli art student attempted to sell art at the residences of a U.S. District Judge and U.S. Magistrate in Baton Rouge, Louisiana. However, according to knowledgeable U.S. government sources, the FBI stayed away from the ongoing DEA-INS investigation for "political reasons."

The Israeli students operated in groups of between 4 to 8 individuals led by "Team Leaders." The team leaders controlled the teams' visits, drove the vehicles, and often had in their vehicles cameras and recording equipment. A number of the students had significant Israeli military experience in demolitions, explosives, and signals intelligence.

The team active in the Irving, Texas area (near Dallas-Fort Worth Airport) had links to the Chesterfield, Missouri-based Israeli communications software firm AMDOCS, which has an outsourcing agreement with Nextel; RETALIX, an Israeli company involved in software for the retail food industry; and NICE, an Israeli software engineering firm. The report cites Michael Calmanovic as the leader of the Irving group and states he "was a recently discharged electronic intercept operator for Israeli military." Calmanovic and his Israeli supervisor from California were arrested on April 4, 2001 in Irving, Texas, while vacating their apartment. The DEA report states Calmanovic used a mailbox drop at Mailboxes, Etc. located at 3575 N. Beltline Rd. Apt. 316, Irving, Texas. The FBI list dated 3 Oct. 2001, which was sent to national financial control authorities to freeze the accounts of the Saudi hijackers and their associates, states the address for suspect Ahmed Khalifa, also known as Almad Khafefa, as 4045 N. Beltline Rd. Apt. 314, Irving, Texas (Marbletree Apartments), just a few blocks from the Israeli mail drop.

There are a number of possible explanations about why the Israeli art students were living so close to the hijackers, especially in Florida where much of the terrorists' flight training occurred. One is that the Israelis had penetrated Al Qaeda with two cells comprising six Egyptian- and Yemeni-born Jews and that some of these agents posed as Israeli art students and were shadowing the Al Qaeda cells inside the United States and reporting their movements back to Mossad or a "cut out" intelligence unit in Ariel Sharon's office. Another explanation is that, like the Israeli "movers" in the New York-New Jersey area, the art students were providing an operational decoy and even material support to the hijackers. This theory arose when several Israeli art students in Canada were arrested for selling bogus Chinese art that they were passing off as Israeli. Two Canadian newspapers reported that U.S. counter-intelligence officials had warned Canadian authorities that the Israeli art students were funneling proceeds from the art sales to

Islamist radical groups.[50] If the Florida and Texas Israeli art rings discovered prior to 911 were providing such financial support to the hijackers, it would explain why they closely located their mail drops so close to one another.

---

[50] Bob Holliday, "Fundamentalist link in cheap art scam?" *Winnipeg Sun*, August 8, 2004, p. 6; Paul Cowan, "Door-To-Door Scam 'Artists' Busted; Local Art Dealers Warn Of Cheap Reproductions," *Edmonton Sun*, August 8, 2004, p. 6.

Chapter 5 -- Mossad's surveillance of domestic U.S. telecommunications

The involvement of the Israeli cells with communications companies raised serious concerns at the DEA and Justice Department, which were both using Israeli communications intercept software in their field operations. The DEA used a T2S2 intercept system provided by Comverse and JSI, two Israeli companies. Comverse was very close to the Israeli government, which reimbursed it up to 50 percent for its research and development costs. The FBI's Communications Assistance to Law Enforcement Act (CALEA) Implementation Office in Chantilly, Virginia was extremely concerned about the threat posed by Comverse's intercept system. But the worries of the Chantilly office and Federal Communications Commission (FCC) were overridden by the FBI's engineering office in Quantico, Virginia, which was supported by such contractors as Booz Allen Hamilton.[51] The nexus of art students, intelligence surveillance, and possible involvement in Ecstasy trafficking set off alarm bells at the highest levels of the DEA about the "art students." The reason was simple. T2S2 systems were used in what the DEA, Coast Guard, Customs, and other counter narcotics agencies called High Intensity Drug Trafficking Areas

---

[51] Carl Cameron, Fox Special Report with Brit Hume, December 13, 2001; Wayne Madsen, "Homeland Security, Homeland Profits," CorpWatch, December 21, 2004.
< http://www.corpwatch.org/issues/PID.jsp?articleid=1108

(HIDTAs) and associated wiretap centers and surveillance teams (STs).

The following internal DEA memo points to the worries about the Israeli systems:

> From: [DELETED]
> Sent: (DELETED]
> To: [DELETED]
> Subject: [DELETED]
>
> I'm not sure what is meant by "Bottom line we should have caught it."
>
> ------Original message-------
> From: Raffanello, Heidi M.
> Sent: Tuesday, December 18, 2001 3:04 PM
> To: Zeisset, Dale M.
> Cc: Newton, Otis L; Howard, JP
> Subject: Comverse
>
> As you may have heard Security Program is briefing the Administrator[52] tomorrow morning on the Israeli students investigation to include T2S2 Comverse and JSI. This was a result of the Fox network expose on Israeli counterintelligence activities. In our discussions about remote maintenance for JSI and Comverse, we realized that Comverse remote maintenance for field systems was not addressed in the C & A process. We will approach it in the similar fashion as we did in the JSI issue, however the foreign national factor doesn't apply. It remains unclear if Comverse personnel are security cleared and if

---

[52] Administrator refers to Asa Hutchinson, the then DEA Administrator. He subsequently was named as the Deputy Secretary of Homeland Security under Secretary Tom Ridge.

so, who are they and what type of clearances are on record. If you have names, I can run their status in Personnel Security. If not, we will need to have Comverse and ST identify a short list of personnel that will require clearances. Obviously, if they have existing clearances with other agencies, this will facilitate the process. Due to the fact that at the time that we conducted the original interim CA for Comverse, the requirements differed than 2640.2D. Bottom line we should have caught it. Please let me know what the status of Comverse remote maintenance past efforts and what direction we need to go to resolve this for CA process. I will have Otis reach out to you to work this out. In light of the Administrator's concern for vulnerabilities to out T2S2 systems, we want to resolve this in time for the January 25th deadline for the review of the conditional.

As of this date, ISI is waiting for the Comverse equipment to arrive at ST so that a C-2 compliance test can be done. Any idea when ST will be in a position to have this done?

On March 4, 2002, Robert F. Diegelman, the acting Assistant Attorney General for Administration, issued a Justice Department memo reiterating that standing Justice Department Order 2640.2D, dated July 12, 2001, prohibited non-U.S. citizens from access to Department of Justice information technology. The order and memo reiterated the policy, "Foreign Nationals shall not be authorized to access or assist in the development, operation, management or maintenance of Department IT systems, unless a waiver has been granted by the Department CIO."

Technology Development Corporation (TDC) was a two-man operation with an Annapolis Junction post office box run by two brothers, Randall and Paul Jacobson of Clarksville, Maryland. After 9/11 and NSA's institution of the STELLAR WIND warrantless telecommunications surveillance program, NSA relied on equipment and software from two Israeli-linked firms. TDC essentially brought Narus, later bought by Boeing, and Verint, owned by Comverse Technology, formerly Comverse Infosys, into the NSA surveillance infrastructure. Both companies were formed by ex-Unit 8200 personnel. Unit 8200, also known as the Israel Signals Intelligence National Unit (ISNU), is the Israeli counterpart of NSA. Paul Jacobson had his security access pulled by NSA in 1992 and he later changed his name to "Jimmy Carter" and "Alfred Olympus von Ronsdorf." It was believed by many senior NSAQ managers that believed that as a result of allowing TDC, Narus, and Verint in the door at NSA, the Israeli government simply passed on NSA technology to Israeli start-up companies that used the NSA-developed know-how to spy on foreign countries, including the United States. In turn, Israel sold the technology back to other countries, including the United States.[53] Astoundingly, that did not prevent him from gaining a super-classified clearance to participate in the NSA program after 9/11.

---

[53] James Bamford, "Shady Companies with Ties to Israel Wiretap the US for NSA," *Wired*, April 3, 2012.

Israel's penetration of NSA was first brought to the attention of the author in June 2005.

One of the firms mentioned as being involved in the security compromise with Israel was CACI, part of an alliance of NSA contractors called the "Eagle Alliance." CACI, called "Colonels and Captains, Inc." by critics who cite the revolving door from the Pentagon to its corporate office suites, counted former NSA Deputy Director Barbara McNamara as a member of its board of directors. CACI alumni also included Thomas McDermott, a former NSA Deputy Director for Information Systems Security. Former NSA Director Adm. Mike McConnell is a Senior Vice President of Booz Allen. CACI's president and CEO Jack London visited Israel in early 2004 and received the Albert Einstein Technology Award at ceremony in Jerusalem attended by Likud Party Defense Minister Shaul Mofaz. The special ceremony honoring CACI's president was sponsored by the Aish HaTorah Yeshiva Fund. The ultra-Orthodox United Torah Judaism Party's Jerusalem Mayor, Uri Lupolianski, was also in attendance.

According to Lebanon's *Daily Star*, CACI's president also met with notorious racist Israeli retired General Effie Eitam who advocates expelling Palestinians from their lands. The U.S. delegation also included a number of homeland security officials, politicians, and businessmen. CACI had received research grants from U.S.-Israeli bi-national foundations.

***

Small teams of Mossad agents found with eavesdropping equipment are nothing new to European or American law enforcement. In

February 1998, five Israelis, three men and two women, were arrested in an apartment in the suburbs of Berne, Switzerland. The Israeli team managed to convince the police that they did not break and enter into the apartment but were there legally. The apartment was the residence of an Islamic activist. Four of the Israelis, two men and two women, were released. However, the fifth Israeli was later discovered with sophisticated surveillance equipment and a number of false passports. He was arrested, detained, and held for 65 days until Israel paid 3 million Swiss francs for his release with a promise he would return from Israel to stand trial. In July 2000, Isaac Bental, the cover name under which the Mossad allowed the Swiss to prosecute their agent, stood trial for espionage before the Swiss Federal Court. It was the first time a Mossad agent had gone on trial outside Israel.[54]

In December 1998, Cypriot police arrested two Israeli agents, Uri Argov and Yisrael Damari, for the illegal possession of communications intercept equipment and espionage. In March 1998, three Mossad agents aborted a wiretapping operation in London after they were tipped off to the police. The Mossad had operated illegally in London since 1987. That year, a furious Margaret Thatcher ordered Israel to close its Palace Green, Kensington Mossad station after its role in the assassination of a Palestinian cartoonist on a South Kensington street was revealed.[55]

---

[54] Swissinfo Web Site, "Swiss court begins hearing charges in case of Israeli secret agent," July 3, 2000.
[55] "Cyprus reportedly refuses to hand over suspected Mossad agents," *Ma'ariv* (Tel Aviv), December 29, 1998; Uzi

In 1999, Shalom Shaphyr, an Israeli national having residences in Vancouver, Washington and Portland, Oregon was arrested by the FBI in Alexandria, Virginia for trying to buy computer intercept equipment from undercover FBI and Customs Service agents. Shaphyr was accused of trying to illegally export the equipment to Vietnam. Shaphyr possessed a business visa that permitted him to enter and leave the United States at will.[56]

On May 31, 2005, it was announced in Israel that Israeli police and Interpol discovered a huge computer espionage ring involving a number of former Israeli intelligence officers and Israeli companies, including AMDOCS. Israeli police questioned AMDOCS computer security manager Eitan Shiron in the investigation that surrounded the use by over a dozen Israeli companies of a sophisticated hacking software program, called a Trojan horse, which bypassed the security controls on targeted computer systems.[57] The Israeli investigation also focused on four major Israeli telecommunications companies – Cellcom, Israel's largest mobile phone company; two subsidiaries of the largest telecommunications company Bezeq Israel Telecom; mobile phone company Pelephone; and satellite television company Yes.[58] Scotland Yard also participated in

Mahnaimi, "Mossad moves to re-open UK spy base," *Sunday Times* (London), April 5, 1998.
[56] "Israeli National Charged in Spy Case," *Sun-Sentinel* (Fort Lauderdale, FL), July 11, 1999.
[57] Noam Sharvit, "AMDOCS exec questioned in industrial espionage," Globes Online (Israel), May 31, 2005 <http://www.globes.co.il/serveen/globes/docview.asp?did=9 19329&fid=942>

the take down of the Israeli espionage ring, arresting dual Israeli-German citizen Michael Haephrati and his wife Ruth Brier-Haephrati in London on an Israeli extradition warrant. The Israeli couple was charged with "unauthorized modification of the contents of a computer" between December 12, 2004 and February 28, 2005." Police said they wrote the Trojan horse computer program and provided it to a middleman. The Trojan horse in question was believed to be a derivative of the PROMIS software program illegally procured from Inslaw, Inc. in Washington, DC in the early 1980s and re-engineered by a number of intelligence agencies, including Israel's, to perform computer espionage. Oddly, *The Scotsman* newspaper reported that Haephrati was questioned about a "separate matter" by detectives with Britain's National Hi-Tech Crime unit on May 25, before his arrest on the Israeli warrant. The Haphraetis were remanded in the Bow Street Magistrates Court in London.[59]

Yet another possible Israeli intelligence link to electronic eavesdropping on the U.S. government was unearthed in the questionable awarding by the U.S. Congress of a wireless contract to a company owned by Israel. In 2000, LGC Wireless, a San Jose, California-based firm was considered in the lead to provide wireless connectivity for the U.S. House of Representatives. A year earlier, the House

---

[58] "Spyware espionage ring cracked; Israeli companies infiltrated by Trojans," Reuters, June 1, 2005.
[59] DEBKAFile Special Update, May 29, 2005; David Stringer, "Israel Extradition: Couple Remanded in Custody," *The Scotsman*, May 26, 2005.

Administration Committee, then headed by Republican Representative Bill Thomas of California, granted LGC authority to conduct a design and security survey of the Capitol. In addition, the FBI and NSA reviewed LGC's system design to ensure that foreign intelligence agencies could not penetrate the House's wireless network. By December 2000, LGC had cleared its plans with the Capitol Architect, the House Information Resource Office, and the House Administration Committee. However, soon a new Israeli company named Foxcom Wireless, which changed its name to MobileAccess, began making an end run to secure the Capitol wireless contract. The new chairman of the House Administration Committee, Republican Representative Bob Ney of Ohio, clearly favored MobileAccess over LGC and in 2002, the Israeli company received the House wireless contract. Ney had a close political and financial relationship with GOP lobbyist Jack Abramoff, an extreme pro-Israeli political insider, who came under Justice Department investigation for questionable ties to Ney and House Majority Leader Tom DeLay. It was later revealed by *The Washington Post* that in 2001 MobileAccess donated $50,000 to the Capital Athletic Foundation, which was run by Abramoff. In 2004, MobileAccess paid $240,000 in lobbying fees to Greenberg Traurig, Abramoff's former firm. The ranking member on the House Administration Committee, Democratic Representative Steny Hoyer of Maryland, said he was not kept fully informed of the wireless contract by either Thomas or Ney. LGC also cried foul when, in 2004, the U.S. Senate awarded MobileAccess a $3.9 million contract to install a wireless network for the Senate.[60] As with the questions surrounding Information Spectrum Inc. abruptly replacing Larimore Associates as the Jersey City Police Department computer system contractor, similar complaints were aired by LGC. Ian Sugarboard, LGC's CEO told *The Hill* newspaper, ". . . it appeared that lobbyists had exerted undue influence on the deal." In addition, the House Administration Committee did not specify what security criteria MobileAccess had to meet. The FBI and NSA had previously approved LGC's security countermeasures.[61]

Abramoff's strong connection to Israel and his influence in the Bush administration serve as yet another nexus between Israel, the Bush administration, and officials closely connected with Saudi Arabia. Top GOP adviser and Abramoff friend Grover Norquist, who was Abramoff's campaign manager when he ran for President of the College Republicans (a post also once held by Karl Rove), also maintained close links to a number of Saudis, some of whom were implicated in funding terrorism. Norquist was a cofounder of the Islamic Institute, co-located in Norquist's Americans for Tax Reform offices in Washington, DC. Norquist was a key player in the Bush 2000 outreach for Muslim and Arab voters. Sami al Arian, a University of South Florida professor, was an ardent supporter of Bush's Florida campaign to woo Muslim and Arab voters and his support likely helped tip the close election to Bush. The Islamic Institute was founded in

---

[60] Patrick O'Connor and Jonathan E, Kaplan, "Wi Fi fight involves Abramoff," *The Hill*, March 3, 2005, p. 11.
[61] Ibid.

1999 with start-up money from Kuwait; Qatar; other Arab countries; the founder of the American Muslim Council, Abdurahman Muhammad Al Amoudi; and two Islamic non-profits, the Safa Trust and the International Institute of Islamic Thought (IIIT). In 2002, as part of OPERATION GREENQUEST, the FBI raided Safa and IIIT for their role in financing international terrorism. Another one of Al Amoudi's groups, the International Relief Organization, was suspected of laundering Saudi money to terrorist groups. Although Arian and Al Amoudi were later charged by the federal government with supporting terrorist groups, they maintained close ties to the Bush campaign. Just a few months before the 911 attacks, Arian attended a June 2001 White house briefing with Karl Rove.

Suhail Khan, the White House point man for arranging access to Bush by prominent Muslim-Americans and a former director of the Islamic Institute, was the son of the late imam of the Santa Clara, California mosque. The mosque had once hosted Dr. Ayman al Zawahiri, the second in command of Al Qaeda. Norquist and his friends were clearly part of a Saudi- and Wahhabi-funded political machine that sought to marginalize moderate Muslims in the United States. Agha Jafri, a Sh'ia leader in New York, said there was in the United States a Saudi "mafia" that was "intent on crushing moderate Sufi and Shiite Muslims in the United States."[62]

---

[62] Mary Jacoby, "Friends in high places; Sami Al-Arian isn't the only prominent Muslim leader who posed for chummy pictures with President Bush. Many conservative Republicans are uneasy at the way GOP power broker

In addition, Norquist's friend Al Amoudi was also discovered to have links to the 911 hijackers. German police files indicated that Al Amoudi met in the fall of 2000 Mohammed Belfas, an Islamic leader in Hamburg who once shared an apartment with Ramzi bin al-Shibh, a kingpin behind the 911 attacks. One of Belfas's colleagues, Agus Budiman, had accompanied Belfas on a scouting mission to Washington, DC in late 2000. Budiman pleaded guilty to helping Belfas obtain a phony identification card using a non-existent address in Arlington, Virginia. German police obtained a photograph from Belfas's Hamburg apartment showing a meeting between him, Budiman, and Al Amoudi in Al Amoudi's Arlington, Virginia office. [63]

Grover Norquist curries support from the Muslim community," *St. Petersburg Times*, March 11, 2003.
[63] Michael Isikoff and mark Hosenball, "Who, and What, Does He Know? New evidence suggests that a leading Muslim spokesman in the U.S. associated with terror suspects," *Newsweek*, October 1, 2003.

Chapter 6 -- The Florida Connection

Texas was not the only case where the Israelis were discovered to be living and working in the same location as the Saudi hijacker cells.

According to the DEA Report, another Israeli team operating out of Hollywood, Florida, led by team leader Hanan Serfaty lived at 4220 Sheridan St., #303, Hollywood, Florida 33021 (Emerald Greens Apartments) while the Saudi hijackers Khalid Al Midhar, Abdulaziz al Omari, Walid Al Shehri, and UAE national Marwan al Shehhi, operated from a mail drop at Mailbox Rentals, 3389 Sheridan St. #256, Hollywood, Florida 33021-3608. Another Serfaty residence at 701 S. 21st Ave., Hollywood was located near the homes of Atta and Al Shehhi, including a residence on Jackson Street, just a few blocks away, and the Bimini Motel Apartments, Apartment 8, at 1600 North Ocean Drive. On September 7, just days before their terrorist attack, Atta and Al Shehhi spent several hours at Shuckums Oyster Bar and Grill at 1814 Harrison St., just a few blocks away from Serfaty's 21st Ave. residence. A Miami-based Israeli unit, led by Legum Yochai, operated from 13753 SW 90th Ave., Miami while hijacker Al Shehri lived nearby at Horizons Apartments, 8025 SW 107th Ave.

During the time the Israelis and Arabs were living in Hollywood, Atta and his team were attending flight training and inquiring about crop dusting planes in southern Florida. According to a source with high-level contacts within the Mossad, Israeli agents based in southern Florida were able to successfully penetrate the Arab cells in southern Florida and informed their Tel Aviv headquarters that an attack on the east coast of the United States was being planned and that it involved commercial aircraft. Although it is not known if these agents were art students, they were Yemeni and Egyptian-born Jews who spoke fluent Arabic and were trained at a secret base in Israel's Negev Desert. Although Mossad chief Efraim Halevy warned CIA Director George Tenet of an "imminent attack," the warning contained no details about the terrorists training on commercial aircraft. Tenet was said to have dismissed the warning because it was not specific. The Mossad units reportedly left the United States after the September 11 attack on El Al flights and were listed on sky marshal manifests as El Al employees.

Venice, Florida is where alleged hijackers Mohammed Atta, Marwan al-Shehhi, and Ziad Jarrah received flight training. The training was extended to Atta and al-Shehhi at Huffman Aviation and to Jarrah at Florida Flight Training Center, both located at Venice Airport. What was once the talk of the town is now hardly mentioned. Venice, which has a population with an average age of 69, went back to being a sleepy retirement community on the shores of the Gulf of Mexico. Here, "9:11" is likely to be a normal evening bedtime rather than a reference to an infamous date in recent U.S. history.

The current residents of the Sandpiper Apartments are, for the most part, unaware that their complex was the focus of an investigation by law enforcement of lead hijacker Mohammed Atta.

A local stripper, Amanda Keller, claimed to have lived in an apartment at the complex from March to April 2001. However, Keller later changed her story and moved away from Venice. Keller can be forgiven for changing her story. While the FBI maintains that Atta was only in Venice attending flight school from July to December 2000 at Huffmann Aviation, which is across the Airport Avenue East from the Sandpiper Apartments, residents of Venice saw Atta in the town in the weeks leading up to 9/11. They recognized his face immediately after it was aired on television following the attacks. From a pharmacist where Atta had prescriptions filled, to a deli counter worker at the Publix supermarket who made Atta his sandwiches, the description was the same: a rude and arrogant man with a glassy stare that indicated he had, somehow, been in a mental institution or "brainwashed."

The apartment, center, upper floor, where Mohammed Atta is said to have lived with

Amanda Kelly in the weeks leading up to 9/11.

Accompanying Atta in the weeks before 9/11 was his father, reportedly a member of the Egyptian Muslim Brotherhood. One Venice resident also claimed that when she was at Maxwell Air Force Base in Alabama, she and her colleagues saw Mohammed Atta, who was wearing the uniform of an Egyptian Air Force colonel.

How did the FBI react to eyewitness claims? They told them they were mistaken. The man they thought was Atta was some other arrogant and wealthy Arab who just happened to be in a community of 10,000 mostly retired people for some unknown reason.

Local townspeople knew Atta was in their town six weeks before 9/11. He had been seen having dinner with Rudi Dekkers, the shady owner of Huffman Aviation. In 1999, Dekkers and his partner, Wally Hilliard, bought Huffman Aviation. According to a Venice CIA source, the choice of Dekkers to be involved in a U.S. and foreign intelligence operation on the scale of 9/11 was unwise. The source said that using a Dutchman in such an operation was "untidy," referring to Dekkers's criminal past in the Netherlands and the CIA's long history with Dutch operatives, who like to get drunk and start talking.

For the 9/11 plotters, Venice was a weak link that could have exposed the entire criminal conspiracy behind 9/11. Atta's noticeable disagreeable public persona, coupled with Dekkers's "untidiness," threatened to link the Venice flight training operation to Governor Jeb Bush in Tallahassee and all the way to the White

House in Washington. Even the Venice police chief posed a problem. He had often said that the police were ordered by the city fathers of Venice never to question or interfere with the operations at the tower-less airport, operations that included Blackhawk helicopters swooping in for only a few seconds, sometimes around 3:00 am, when they would pick up or discharge passengers. The political leadership of Venice was beholden to the man who was heavily invested in the town: Jackson Stephens, the billionaire Little Rock, Arkansas tycoon who had helped bankroll the presidential campaigns of Bill Clinton and George W. Bush.

Venice Municipal Airport was used by the military during World War II as a base. But it was not just any regular base, it was used by the Office of Strategic Services (OSS), the forerunner of the CIA, to train Nationalist Chinese pilots to fight against the Japanese. The operation was overseen by General Claire Chennault, to founder of the Flying Tigers that assisted Chiang Kai-shek's forces before and during America's entry into World War II. Chennault was also a founder of the Civil Air Patrol, which is headquartered at Maxwell Air Force Base. Chennault was a supporter of the Louisiana Civil Air Patrol, which once counted James Bath, George W. Bush's Texas Air National Guard friend; Drug Enforcement Administration informant and pilot Barry Seal; alleged John F. Kennedy assassination conspirator David Ferrie; and accused Kennedy assassin Lee Harvey Oswald as members.

Huffman Aviation, once the interest of the FBI, with a new identity: Suncoast Air Center.

Today, Amanda Keller has moved away to start a new life. Huffman Aviation was bought and now the building is called "Suncoast Air Center." Huffman's original corporate records have disappeared into an administrative "black hole." And Venice has returned to a sleepy retirement community.[64]

An investigation of accused 9/11 hijacker Mohammed Atta's whereabouts prior to the September 11, 2001, terrorist attacks strongly indicate that he was sent to Key West, Florida in order to provide a plausible cover story about his passport that would be provided to the media following the attacks.

New York Police Commissioner Bernard Kerik reported to CBS's News's Scott Pelley that "one of the hijackers'" passports was found 3 to 4

---

[64] August 15-16, 2012, "Cleaning up the 9/11 evidence and clues in Florida," WayneMadsenReport.com.

blocks away from the debris from the collapsed World Trade Center. It was later reported that the passport was in pristine condition and managed to survive that way in explosive temperatures that incinerated the hijacked American Airlines Boeing 767's "black boxes" and melted steel in the World Trade Center. It was also later reported that the pristine passport belonged to another hijacker, Satam al-Suqumi, and was found by a "pedestrian." It should be kept in mind that for weeks after 9/11, only authorized individuals were permitted near "Ground Zero." Unauthorized persons were not permitted to go south beyond 34th Street.

It was also reported that a "Mohamed Atta" (there are a number of transliterations of Arabic names into English and Mohamed is often interchanged with Mohammed and Muhammad) traveled on a novelty passport issued by the Conch Republic, a fantasy nation that was established as a protest in 1982 by the Florida Keys to the creation of a detached U.S. border station on U.S. Highway 1 in Florida City, just south of Homestead, to check for illegal aliens heading north from the Keys. The people of the Keys decided if they were going to be treated like foreigners, they would secede from the United States. The border check was finally removed but the Conch Republic lived on, not so much as a political protest, but as a humorous symbolic republic that worked in tandem with the Chamber of Commerce of the Keys and the municipal government of Key West to promote tourism and the uniqueness of the Florida Keys. The mayor of Key West also serves as the "prime minister" of the Conch Republic.

106

But the humor of the Conch Republic and the novelty passports it issues was seemingly lost on some individuals who, in September 2000, began applying for the novelty passports from locations in Pakistan, India, and the United Arab Emirates. The sudden spate of such requests led officials of the Conch Republic to notify the immigration and Naturalization Service (INS) in Miami of a potential problem with people who might be trying to enter the United States illegally by using the novelty passports. The INS never responded but the Conch Republic drafted a letter for the record that such a report was made to the INS.

In February 2001, Mohamed Atta and his stripper/lingerie model girlfriend, Amanda Keller, were spotted all over Key West. They were seen at the Red Garter, a notorious Key West strip club; the Hard Rock Cafe; and Sloppy Joe's, the name of the haunt where novelist Ernest Hemingway drank and, on occasion, pointed out to his friends the FBI agents who were in the bar watching him.

But while Hemingway drew the interest of the FBI, the bureau had no similar interest in Atta. It was while Atta and Keller were at the Hard Rock Cafe that Atta left to pick up a mysterious German-speaking man who arrived at Key West International Airport. The German-speaking man stayed with Atta and his girlfriend for a few days. After a few days, Atta, Keller, and the German left Key West. There have been some reports that the German man was Wolfgang Bohringer, a Swiss-German who tried to establish a flight school in Kiribati in the South Pacific but was asked to leave by that nation's president. Bohringer has been rumored to be a longtime CIA asset from the shady ranks of the agency that have also reportedly included Rudi Dekkers, the owner of Huffman Aviation, the Venice, Florida flight school where Atta was enrolled.

After 9/11, two FBI agents arrived at the door of the Conch Republic, located in a traditional Key West wood-frame house on Simonton Street, a block away from the tourist shops and bars on Duval Street. It was clear that the agents were there because of what was allegedly "found" in the rubble in New York: a passport issued in September 2000 to a Mohamed Atta, who applied for it using a New York City mailing address. The FBI was told that the Conch Republic was suspicious about some passport requests received the previous year from the Middle East and Indian sub-continent and that the information was conveyed to the INS without a response.

The Conch Republic voluntarily turned over to the FBI agents bankers' boxes containing some 25,000 Conch Republic passport applications, including addresses, telephone numbers, copies of supporting identification documents, and even the DNA from licked envelopes and postage stamps. It was from these files that an application from a "Mohamed Atta" in New York was discovered, but the FBI presumably already knew that from what was found in perfect shape in the debris of the World Trade Center. Instead of keeping the information about Atta secure, the FBI leaked the Conch Republic passport application information to the *Miami Herald.* The paper dispatched reporter Jennifer Babson to Key West to interview Conch Republic Secretary General Peter Anderson.

Babson asked Anderson why Atta "had been using a Conch Republic passport to travel." In fact, there was never any evidence that Atta had personally possessed such a passport, let alone having traveled on one.

The *Herald's* FBI source or sources were not truthful in what they passed on to the paper, information that was repeated in Babson's October 3, 2001, article: the article states that "Mohamed Atta" signed the Conch Republic's registration book at their Key West headquarters (currently, visits to the headquarters are by appointment and walk-ins are not permitted). However, the Herald reported that agents were unable to find Atta's passport application in the 25,000 files. WMR has been told that there was such an application and it was mailed from New York City, where there was never any record of the alleged hijacker Atta having had a permanent mailing address.

There are strong suspicions by informed parties in Key West that someone else applied for the Conch Republic passport using the name Mohamed Atta and when the time was right, the passport was dropped into the debris on Vesey Street near the Trade Center site. In turn, the passport was handed to Kerik.

Kerik, who served a prison term after a federal corruption conviction, never revealed who gave him the passport in question. Sources revealed to the author that Kerik expressed fear that he spoke too much about the details of 9/11, he would be placed in the general prison population -- a virtual death sentence for a police officer -- rather than in the minimum security prison where he is now serving out his term.

109

Atta's only known passport was his Egyptian passport, number 1617066, with a U.S. B1/B2 visa, number 34137932, issued at the U.S. embassy in Berlin on May 18, 2000.

The visit by the two FBI agents, supervisory resident agent Rae Bliss and her deputy Anthony Russo, to the Conch Republic office on suspicion that Atta may have used a novelty passport is not supported by the conclusions of the 9/11 Commission, which stated: "The FBI and CIA have uncovered no evidence that Atta held any fraudulent passports." WMR learned that FBI agent Bliss's husband was, at the time of the investigation, a CIA officer assigned to the Joint Task Force-Key West, a component of the U.S. Southern Command in Miami. Bliss and her husband are now retired.

Those familiar with Atta's Key West visit in February 2001, said he possessed a number of passports and spoke a number of languages, including Hebrew. In fact, it was discovered in 2001 that a number of Israel Defense Force reservists operated many of the small boutique shops in Key West, which sold everything from skin lotions and children's toys to jewelry and kitschy souvenirs. The IDF vendors, according to our sources, periodically flew back and forth to Israel in the months leading up to 9/11.[65]

---

[65] August 20-21, 2012, "Mohammed Atta's mysterious passport," WayneMadsenReport.com

Chapter 7 -- Israeli Foreknowledge of 9/11

It is likely that some of the Mossad warnings about hijackings in the United States did reach some people. Officials at Odigo, an instant-messaging company with offices in New York and Herzliya (where the headquarters of Mossad is located) admitted that two of its employees said they received e-mail warning of the attack two hours before the planes careened into the twin towers. Alex Diamandis, Odigo's vice president for sales and marketing, confirmed that Odigo employees in New York and Israel received a warning two hours before the attack. The warning appeared to be anonymous but Odigo programmers recorded the Internet protocol address of the message's sender. Odigo also notified Mossad and the FBI but the FBI failed to take action and notify occupants of the World Trade Center.[66]

By September 3, 2001, Zim-American Israeli Shipping Company, completed its move from the World Trade Center to Norfolk, Virginia after suddenly canceling its lease in April 2001 and forfeiting a $50,000 lease cancellation penalty. World Trade Center and New York-New Jersey Port Authority Police had previously determined that Zim's World Trade Center office was an intelligence operation that involved Mossad and CIA agents. Unlike other tenants in

---

[66] Brian McWilliams, "Instant Messages To Israel Warned Of WTC Attack," Newsbytes, September 27, 2001.

the World Trade Center, Zim's stairwell access door were covered by security cameras.[67]

The major media largely failed to report the story of Israeli intelligence teams masquerading as art students. Only Fox News referred to it in a four-part investigative series in December 2001 but soon removed it from its web site. At the time, reporter Carl Cameron stated, "There is no indication that the Israelis were involved in the September 11 attacks, but investigators suspect that the Israelis may have gathered intelligence about the attacks in advance, and not shared it."[68]

However, Cameron's report was somewhat bolstered by news reports in early 2002 that Mossad chief Efraim Halevy, in early September 2001, sent the CIA a warning of an impending Arab terrorist attack on the East Coast of the United States. Two three- man Mossad units consisting of Yemeni- and Egyptian-born Jews had apparently tracked some of the September 11 hijackers in Hamburg and south Florida. CIA chief George Tenet referred to the Mossad report as "too non-specific" and decided not to order any higher alert level throughout the CIA's network of stations. Follow-up reports from the Mossad units referred to their quarry attending flight training. After the attacks, the Mossad teams left the United States on board El Al flights.[69]

---

[67] Confidential information from World Trade Center and New York-New Jersey Port Authority Police.
[68] Carl Cameron, Fox Special Report with Brit Hume, December 11, 2001.
[69] Gordon Thomas, "Bush: The Ignored Warning That Will Come to Haunt Him," Globe-Intel, May 21, 2002.
<http://www.gordonthomas.ie/104.html>

Newspapers across the United States also reported Israelis being arrested around U.S. military installations. In May 2001, two Israelis, Gal Kantor and Tsvi Watermann, were arrested at the Volk Field Air National Guard base at Camp Douglas in Juneau County, Wisconsin. They said they were going to visit a museum on the base but instead began taking photographs on the runway. When an Air Force security guard asked the young men if they were selling art, Kantor became upset and demanded to know why the question was being asked. Obviously, the Volk Field security personnel had been warned about the suspicious activities of Israeli art students. Three days before the two Israelis were arrested at Volk Field, four Israelis were arrested and deported after they were discovered selling art door-to-door in a neighborhood close to Tinker Air Force Base in Oklahoma. Reflecting some sort of official sensitivity about the Volk Field incident, the base sent a news release to the *Capital Times* of Madison marked "for release on request only."[70]

The Tinker Air Force Base incident was confirmed by Midwest City Police Chief Brandon Clabes who said his police officers "were on alert" because they received a national security advisory warning that "Israeli nationals were posing as students selling artwork... to gain information about the U.S. military and security." Clabes said his officers encountered the Israelis on May 17, 2002, shortly after 7:15 PM. Two of the Israelis were on foot conducting "unusual door-to-door solicitations" in the Oakwood East housing area.

---

[70] Doug Moe, "Israeli Spies Lurking in State?" *The Capital Times*, May 10, 2002, p. 2A.

A third Israeli was acting as a driver. In addition to several other photo identification cards, all three had Israeli Air Force identification. Clabes identified the three Israelis as Naor Topaz, Zeev Cahen, and Yaron Ohana. The three Israelis and a fourth member of their team were later arrested by the police on visa violations. The Israelis denied they were selling their artwork. Although the Air Force Office of Special Investigations later denied the Israelis were involved in espionage, Clabes said higher authorities in U.S. law enforcement believed the Israelis were using the selling of art to get people to divulge additional information by first engaging in "casual conversation about art, and then start slipping in questions about who lived there, is their family in the military--those types of things."[71]

Around 8:10 AM on September 11, 2001, American Airlines flight attendant Madeline Amy Sweeney, a 13-year veteran of the airline, used her cell phone to report to her supervisor at Logan Airport in Boston about the hijacking and murders occurring on her aircraft. A Federal Aviation Administration (FAA) Memorandum written the same day stated that one of the hijackers assigned to seat 10B (reportedly Satam Al Suqami) shot and killed the passenger assigned to seat 9B. The passenger shot was reported to have been Daniel C. Lewin, an Israeli-American agent with the top secret Israeli anti-terrorist Unit 269 of the counter-terrorism Sayeret Matkal branch of the Israeli Defense Force. Lewin also served as the chief technology officer of Akamai Technologies, Inc.,

---

[71] Randy Ellis, "Four Israelis deported after Tinker incident," *Daily Oklahoman*, March 8, 2002.

114

a software company based in Cambridge, Massachusetts.[72] The 911 Commission Report stated that Lewin was stabbed and not shot by Suqami. While Lewin and Israel were praised in the report no mention was made of Sweeney's last words to her superiors.

The FAA Memo, which was later reported by the FAA to be alternately erroneous and a first draft, was eventually scrubbed from the FAA's internal e-mail system. The original FAA memo stated:

EXECUTIVE SUMMARY
September 11, 2001

On September 11, 2001, several commercial air carrier incidents, believed to be terrorist-related, occurred in various locations in the United States. As numerous U.S. passenger air carriers were involved, this has impacted many passengers as well as numerous persons on the ground in these various crash sites. The following is a summary of the events, which have occurred:

American Airlines Flight 11, departed today from Boston Logan International Airport (BOS), bound for Los Angeles International Airport (LAX). The aircraft type was a Boeing 767-200 with eighty-one passengers, nine flight attendants and two crew in the cockpit, which totaled 92 persons on this flight. At approximately 9:18 AM, it was reported that the two crew members in the cockpit were

---

[72] UPI Hears, March 2, 2002.
<http://www.upi.com/view.cfm?StoryID=06032002-121706-8744r>

stabbed. The flight then descended with no communication from the flight crew members. The American Airlines FAA Principle Security Inspector (PSI) was notified by Suzanne Clark of American Airlines Corporate Headquarters, that an on board flight attendant contacted American Airlines Operations Center and informed that a passenger located in seat 10B shot and killed a passenger in seat 9B at 9:20 AM.[73] The passenger killed was Daniel Lewin, shot by passenger Satam Al Suqami. One bullet was reported to have been fired. The flight headed in the direction of John F. Kennedy International Airport (JFK). At 9:25 AM, this flight crashed directly into one of the towers at the World Trade Center. At 11:26 AM, a passenger manifest was obtained. The status of any selectees is as yet undetermined.

United Airlines Flight 93 departed this morning, from Newark International Airport (EWR) bound for San Francisco International

---

[73] The 9:20 AM entry was an obvious typographic error and likely should have been 8:20 AM because at 8:46 AM, Flight 11 crashed into the North Tower of the World Trade Center. The shooting of Lewin at 8:20 AM was simultaneous to the time that Logan Airport flight control determined that Flight 11 had been hijacked. A gunshot report by the flight attendant may have contributed to that determination since all communications with the cockpit had ceased at around 8:15 AM. The FAA memo was prepared at 5:31 PM Eastern Daylight Time at the end of a working day when most of Washington's government employees had evacuated the city in panic and confusion; ABC News Prime Time Thursday, "Calm Before the Crash Flight 11 Crew Sent Key Details Before Hitting the Twin Towers," July 18, 2002.
<http://abcnews.go.com/sections/primetime/DailyNews/prim etime_flightattendants_020718.html>

Airport (SFO). The aircraft type is Boeing 757, confirmation pending. The flight consisted of thirty-eight passengers, two pilots and five crew members, which totaled 45 persons on this flight. Two selectee passengers (Christine Adams and Nicole Miller) were boarded on this flight with no unusual behavior noted per the air carrier personnel and screeners.[74] No cargo was on board this flight. One unit load device (ULD), was on board containing U.S. mail. At 9:42 AM, there was a report of a bomb threat on board this flight. Passengers' screams were heard in the cabin. At 10:05 AM, the Illinois State Police received a 9-1-1 telephone call from a passenger on that flight, who reported that three hijackers were on board with knives and reportedly made a bomb threat. The three hijackers were reported to be rushing to the cockpit area. At 10:12 AM, the flight crashed near Somerset, PA. This location is approximately 70-90 miles from Pittsburgh near Route 30.

United Airlines Flight 175, departed from Boston-Logan International Airport (BOS), bound for Los Angeles International Airport (LAX). This aircraft type was a Boeing 767. There were no selectee passengers on this flight. The flight consisted of nine crew members and forty-seven passengers, which

---

[74] Under the Computer-Assisted Passenger Pre-Screening System (CAPPS), "selectee passengers" were those subject to additional security screening. A selectee passenger was identified based on a lack of knowledge about him or her, use of cash to pay for a ticket, and other parameters. While two women with common names, Adams and Miller, were "selected," the hijackers apparently boarded Flight 93 without any arousal of suspicion.

totaled fifty-six persons on this flight. At 9:30 AM, radar contact with FAA air traffic control was lost. At 9:45 AM, United Airlines reported that one flight attendant was stabbed and two crew members were killed. This flight crashed into the second World Trade Center Tower.

Page 2

American Airlines Flight 77, departed Washington-Dulles International Airport (IAD), destined for Los Angeles International Airport (LAX). This flight departed Gate D26 of the IAD mid-field terminal at 8:09 a.m., and was airborne at 8:21 AM. The aircraft type was a Boeing 757. Number of selectee passengers is unknown at this time; ramp personnel noticed two selectees checked bags on the ramp. One non-selectee passenger did not board due to confusion of gate location. This flight consisted of fifty-eight passengers and six flight crew members, which totaled sixty-four persons on this flight. There was no cargo being transported on this aircraft. There were a total of thirty-five checked bags. It is presumed that this flight crashed into the Pentagon located in Washington, DC at approximately 10:00 AM.

Additional information is continuously being gathered on each of the four incidents described above.

911/01 5:31 PM

In November 2001, the INS arrested several Israelis, including some with military backgrounds, selling Puzzle Car and Zoom Copter

118

toys from shopping mall kiosks and vending carts. Many of the malls were located near U.S. government facilities, including the Pentagon and CIA. A majority of the Israelis, arrested for visa violations instead of espionage, worked for a Florida-based company called Quality Sales. A spokesman for the company admitted the company hired vacationing Israeli students but they had the wrong visas. The spokesman also revealed the Israelis were deemed "special interest" cases by INS – a new government designation applied to terrorism suspects in the wake of 911.[75] Federal authorities suspect the Israelis were using the kiosks as intelligence fronts in the same manner that Israelis were using door-to-door art sales as covers. The National Counterintelligence Center (NCIX) stated in a report issued in March 2001 that, "In the past six weeks, employees in federal office buildings located throughout the United States have reported suspicious activities connected with individuals representing themselves as foreign students selling or delivering artwork. Employees have observed both males and females attempting to bypass facility security and enter federal buildings." The report was temporarily removed from the NCIX web site.

One of the malls where the Israeli "toy sellers" based their operations was the Pentagon City Mall, just across Interstate 395 from the Pentagon. In July 2004, the mall served as the rendezvous point for alleged Israeli Pentagon spy Larry Franklin and Keith Weissman, an AIPAC official. Franklin warned Weissman that Iranian agents were going to start attacking American

---

[75] Saunders, op. cit.

soldiers and Israeli agents in Iraq. Weissman then went to brief the account of the meeting to Steve Rosen, another senior AIPAC official. They both informed the Israeli embassy in Washington and Glenn Kessler, a reporter for *The Washington Post*. Those phone calls were being wiretapped by the FBI as part of its investigation of a major Israeli spy ring in the United States, an investigation that had been going on since before the 911 attacks. The FBI was also monitoring meetings between Franklin, Weissman, and Rosen, including one held in February 2003 at the Arlington, Virginia Ritz-Carlton hotel, which adjoins the Pentagon City Mall. [76]

In February 2005, an Israeli man named Ohad Cohen was deported, along with four other Israelis, from Omaha, Nebraska. In what was becoming a common occurrence in the United States, a total of ten Israelis, who were working at shopping mall kiosks in the Omaha and Lincoln areas, were deported by Immigration and Customs Enforcement officials for illegally working in the United States on tourist visas. The Israelis operated out of Omaha's Oak View Mall and Lincoln's Gateway Westfield Mall. The Federal government probe was reported to be part of a wider probe of Israeli shopping mall kiosk activity throughout the Midwest. In December 2004, FBI and immigration officers arrested 15 Israelis in Minnesota and three operating from a mall kiosk in Grand Forks, North Dakota.[77] Omaha is also the

---

[76] Jerry Markon, "FBI Tapped Talks About Possible Secrets," *The Washington Post*, June 3, 2005, p. A07.
[77] Cindy Gonzalez, "Mall kiosk probe ends in Israelis' deportation," *Omaha World Herald*, February 9, 2005, p.

headquarters of the U.S. Air Force Strategic Air Command (SAC).

The International Association of Counter-terrorism and Security Professionals wrote in a May 2000 report that "U.S. law enforcement reports 'numerous encounters' with Middle Eastern 'art students' with 'fraudulent documents' who attempted to 'gain unauthorized access' to federal buildings."[78]

The unusual casing of sensitive locations continued after 9/11. According to informed sources in Corpus Christi, Texas, young Israelis were seen conducting surveillance of the Port of Corpus Christi in January 2002. The report was contained in the U.S. Coast Guard's Corpus Christi Marine Safety Office Intelligence Bulletin. The bulletin stated:

> ...There were four significant events in the Port of Corpus Christi in the past four weeks. Each event is under current investigation by the FBI. They may or may not be cases of actual or potential surveillance.
>
> ➢ Three men of Middle Eastern descent on board a charter boat in Port Aransas were asking unusual and very nosy questions about the operation of the ship's machinery and equipment.

5B; Cindy Gonzalez, "Mall kiosk probe ends in Israelis' deportation An Israeli man was accused of using illegal "tourist" workers," *Omaha World-Herald*, February 8, 2005, p. 5B.
[78] Werner, op. cit.

- Five men of Middle Eastern descent taking photographs of the Clark Flagship charter boat at 11:30 at night.
- A man and a woman of Middle Eastern descent were taking pictures outside the fence of Citgo East. Upon questioning by security personnel, the female stated they were art students. She further added they were photographing a "pipe rack." The term is one that would only be used by someone in the industry. Coupled along with several other suspicious indicators, the picture taking did not seem legitimate.
- Two men of Middle Eastern descent drove through a gate at Citgo West after it was opened to let a delivery truck out. The men drove straight down to the oil docks where a ship was moored. Before security personnel could arrive, the men boarded the ship for several minutes, and were en-route back out of the facility. The men claimed to be selling electronic equipment. In a search of their truck by the sheriff's office, a loaded pistol was found in the cab. They had also been denied access at an adjacent facility shortly before this incident.[79]

The FBI investigated a case of a "Middle Eastern-looking" man photographing the Ultramar Diamond Shamrock refinery in Three Rivers, Texas, near Corpus Christi. On November 22, 2001, a refinery employee saw the man taking pictures from Highway 281. The man sped away when refinery employees approached his vehicle, a Dodge van rented from McAllen, Texas. The FBI was called in to investigate. Live Oak County Sheriff Larry Busby said the FBI never followed up with his office after the incident. Busby and Three Rivers police chief Ace Robbins had been on the alert ever since September 11 when a suspicious aircraft was seen circling the Ultramar refinery.[80]

In June 2004, groups of young and neatly dressed "Middle Eastern-looking" men were also spotted near the U.S.-Mexican border in Arizona's Cochise County near Tombstone and the U.S. Army Intelligence and Security Command at Fort Huachuca. A spokesman for the U.S. Border Patrol in Tucson said he was not at liberty to discuss the country of origin of the Middle Eastern-looking men.[81] According to FBI sources,

[79] U.S. Coast Guard Marine Safety Office, Corpus Christi, *Intelligence Bulletin*, TIN #7, January 17, 2002.

[80] J. R. Gonzalez, "FBI is looking into person taking photos of refinery; snapping pictures is fairly common, authorities say; patrols increased since man spotted doing so Nov. 22," *Corpus Christi Caller Times*, December 14, 2001, p. B1.

[81] "Two Groups of Middle Eastern Invaders Caught in Cochise County in Past Six Weeks," *Tombstone Tumbleweed*, < http://www.tombstonetumbleweed.com/tombstone/default.asp#iframe1>

"Middle Eastern-looking" or "Middle Eastern descent" are internal code word used to describe Israelis without having to face the inevitable political problems of identifying them as such.

Copies of Department of Homeland Security morning briefs, classified "For Official Use Only," were mistakenly leaked to the public from an Energy Department web site. The briefs contain a number of references to suspicious "Middle East looking" persons seen around sensitive U.S. facilities. The descriptions match identically the behavior of Israeli "art students" cited in the DEA Report and various other law enforcement encounters with Israeli "movers."

The September 27, 2004 brief stated:

FOUO) MAINE: Suspicious Persons in Southwest Harbor. According to 23 September USCG reporting, a concerned citizen reported suspicious behavior by three men of possible Middle Eastern descent at a convenience store located in Southwest Harbor. The men were asking if any local businesses rented power boats, kayaks, or bikes. The men were driving a maroon-colored van with Florida license plates. The reporting citizen stated that although he initially thought the men's behavior was suspicious, he did not think to report it, until he learned that the Queen Mary II would be making a port visit to Bar Harbor on 27 September. An investigation is ongoing. (COGARD Southwest Harbor; 23 Sep 04; HSOC 3577-04)

MASSACHUSETTS: Possible Video Surveillance of Interstate Highway. According to military reporting, on 22 September, in Lexington, a military member reported observing four Middle Eastern individuals standing on an I-95 overpass videotaping the northbound traffic and recording information into a notebook. Reportedly, the same military member recalled observing two of the individuals on the same overpass in late February or early March 2004. (AFOSI Talon 102-23-09-04-2297; 23 Sep 04; HSOC 3579-04)[82]

From the September 29, 2004 briefing there were additional reports of suspicious "Middle Easterners," in addition to a report from San Francisco about suspicious activity by two individuals whose van was traced to a jewelry store in Seattle:

FLORIDA: Suspicious Photographing and Videotaping of High-Rise Buildings Including the Main Street Bridge and the Skyway. According to 25 September Jacksonville Regional Domestic Security Task Force reporting, in downtown Jacksonville, an off-duty police officer reported seeing one of three people, whom he described as Middle Eastern in appearance, photographing and videotaping high-rise buildings, to include the Main Street Bridge and the Skyway. When the off-duty police officer pulled alongside the minivan, the individual with the camera immediately put it down, and the minivan departed the area. The off-duty police officer reported the minivan's license plate and description. The registration showed the minivan was maroon, while the vehicle the officer saw appeared gray. An investigation is on-going. (FDLE Daily Brief, 28 Sep 04; HSOC 3629-04)

(FOUO) WASHINGTON / CALIFORNIA: Suspicious Activity at USCG Group San Francisco. According to USCG reporting, on 23 September, Coast Guard members observed two individuals in a blue van

---

[82] Homeland Security, Homeland Security Operations Center, Homeland Security Operations Morning Brief, 27 September 2004.

taking pictures of the Bay Bridge and surrounding area in front of USCG Group San Francisco's main gate. The license plates were traced to a jewelry store address in Seattle, Washington. Additional checks revealed that the two individuals were not owners, employed or had any association with the store. An investigation is on-going. (COGARD San Francisco, 28 Sep 04; HSOC 3630-04)[83]

From the September 30, 2004, Homeland Security brief, there were further descriptions of "Middle Eastern" activity:

FOUO) WASHINGTON: Suspicious Activity of Two Middle Eastern Males on Ferry. According to USCG reporting, on 27 September, in Seattle, two Middle Eastern males were observed studying the schematic of the Wenatchee Ferry for an extended period of time. As soon as the two males noticed an employee approaching, they immediately walked away from the schematic and picked up a magazine to ward off attention. At the end of the voyage, the two males returned to their vehicle. A license plate check revealed the vehicle belonged to a rental company. Information from the rental company on the vehicle indicated that it was a rented to a business located in Tukwila. The business was unable to be located. An investigation is on-going. (COGARD FIST Seattle, 28 Sep 04; HSOC 3657-04)[84]

On October 14, 2004, a further report on "Middle Eastern" activity:

---

[83] Homeland Security, Homeland Security Operations Center, Homeland Security Operations Morning Brief, 29 September 2004.
[84] Homeland Security, Homeland Security Operations Center, Homeland Security Operations Morning Brief, 30 September 2004.

Suspicious Activity at Andrews AFB Main Gate.
According to military reporting, on 12 October,
Andrews AFB security officers observed a possible
Middle Eastern male photographing the main gate area
using what appeared to be a small, disposable camera.
When a security officer approached the individual to
question him, the unidentified male left the gate area,
walked across the street, met up with another
individual believed to also be of Middle Eastern origin,
entered a white, late-model Pontiac Grand Am and
quickly departed the area. Reportedly, a possible
Middle Eastern female was sitting in the back of the
vehicle. (AFOSI Talon 331-12-10-04-2484, 12 Oct 04;
HSOC 3876-04)[85]

A particularly suspicious report was found in the
October 19, 2004 brief. Several teams of Israeli art
students had cased U.S. Air Force bases, including
Tinker Air Force Base in Oklahoma City:

MISSOURI: Suspicious Telephone Calls. According
to military reporting, on 15 October, at Whiteman Air
Force Base [home base for the B-2 bomber], an
unknown male, described as having a heavy Middle
Eastern accent, telephonically contacted the 509 th
Munitions Squadron, claiming that he represented a
not-for-profit organization and wanted to confirm the
squadron's address. Reportedly, when questioned
about his organization, the unknown caller became
belligerent and ended the phone call. On 16 October,
another member of the 509th Munitions Squadron
received a call at his residence on his personal cellular
telephone from an unknown individual—also described

---

[85] Homeland Security, Homeland Security Operations
Center, Homeland Security Operations Morning Brief, 14
October 2004.

as having a Middle Eastern accent—who solicited information related to Whiteman AFB, where the military member worked, and other operationally related questions. The military member did not provide any information to the caller and hung up. An investigation is on-going. (USAF Talon Report, 207-18-10-04-2533, 18 Oct 04; HSOC 3953-04)[86]

From the October 26, 2004 brief:

(FOUO) ILLINOIS: Possible Surveillance Activity. According to the Illinois State Terrorism Intelligence Center (STIC), on 22 October, in Joliet, at a worksite at the McDonough Street Bridge, a construction foreman observed a male of possible Middle Eastern origin taking photographs of the bridge. When the foreman told the unidentified male to leave, the individual became upset and continued to photograph nearby buildings before departing the area. Reportedly, the individual left in a Chevrolet Cavalier with Minnesota plates which have been traced back to a finance company in Boca Raton, Florida. (Illinois State Police STIC, 25 Oct 04; HSOC 4065-04)[87]

From the December 9, 2004 brief yet another incident involving a U.S. Air Force Base:

TEXAS: DoD Lesson Plans Stolen from USAF Member Hotel Room / Possible Surveillance Activities. According to 7 December military reporting, in San Antonio at Lackland AFB, on 30 November, USAF personnel arrived at a local hotel

---

[86] Homeland Security, Homeland Security Operations Center, Homeland Security Operations Morning Brief, 19 October 2004.
[87] Homeland Security, Homeland Security Operations Center, Homeland Security Operations Morning Brief, 26 October 2004.

and noticed four possible Middle Eastern males behaving suspiciously. Approximately three to four days later, the men were observed counting and photographing the doors to the rooms belonging to the USAF members. Reportedly, the men always traveled together, and appeared to be purposely present when the USAF members gathered for breakfast. The men were also noted to have the "No Service" door magnets posted on their doors throughout the day. On 6 December, one USAF member reported that his lesson plans were stolen from his room. The other USAF members reported that nothing was missing, but personal items were seemingly out of place in their rooms to include open drawers and closet doors. An investigation is on-going. (AFOSI Talon #409-07-12-04-2968, 7 Dec 04; HSOC 4701-04)[88]

Another suspicious case was reported in the December 28, 2004 briefing involving two "Middle Easterners" with Florida connections:

(FOUO) NEW JERSEY: Suspicious Activity at Critical Infrastructure. According to a Call-in report, on 20 December, at a Dam in Morris County, a Vehicle occupied by two males of possible Middle Eastern descent entered a restricted area. A Dam employee approached the vehicle and advised the subjects that they were on private property. The two subjects claimed that they wanted to take one last look at the reservoir and dam before they relocated to Florida. The Dam employee ordered the subjects to leave the premises, informing them that local law enforcement had been contacted. The vehicle took off at a high rate of speed leaving the premises. (Call in, 27 December 04: HSOC 4929-04)[89]

---

[88] Homeland Security, Homeland Security Operations Center, Homeland Security Operations Morning Brief, 9 December 2004.

The December 30, 2004 brief actually contained a report concerning Israeli-Ukrainians detained in Buffalo for passport fraud:

(FOUO) NEW YORK: Ukrainian Nationals Attempt Entry with Photo-Substituted Passports and Visas. According to BTS reporting, on 29 December, Ukrainian nationals Ivan SERNOWSKIY (DOB: 10/25/1968, A97914917) and Maria FESTUK (DOB: 06/20/1975, A97914918) arrived by bus at the Buffalo, NY Port of Entry (POE) claiming to be an Israeli couple named Vyesheslav and Marya URMANOV. The couple applied for admission as visitors for pleasure. SERNOWSKIY presented Israeli passport 8400058 in the name of Vyesheslav URMANOV (DOB: 03/12/1965) with a visa issued in Tel Aviv on November 29, 2000 (foil 41200881). FESTUK presented Israeli passport 6830276 in the name of Marya URMANOV (DOB: 06/20/1975) with machine-readable visa (20011717790001). The Automated Biometrics Identification System (IDENT) checks resulted in a fingerprint mismatch on Mr. URMANOV. The couple was referred to secondary for further examination. NTC research revealed a recent photo of Vyesheslav URMANOV which was forwarded to CBP officers for comparison. SERNOWSKIY was confronted with the fingerprint and photograph discrepancies and admitted his true identity. The U.S. Attorney's Office accepted this case for prosecution. CBP determined both aliens were inadmissible to the U.S. (willful misrepresentation of material fact), refused their admission, and detained them for prosecution. (BTS Daily Operations Report, 30 Dec 04; HSOC 4958-04)

---

[89] Homeland Security, Homeland Security Operations Center, Homeland Security Operations Morning Brief, 28 December 2004.

The December 30 brief also included a report reminiscent of Israeli art student surveillance of Federal buildings and offices:

(FOUO) MARYLAND: Possible Surveillance of Federal Building in Baltimore. According ICE reporting 28 December, a Special Agent from the US Department of Housing and Urban Development, Office of Inspector General (HUD-OIG) observed three individuals conducting possible surveillance of two federal facilities in Baltimore, MD. The two male and one female subjects, described as being of Middle Eastern descent, were seen videotaping the US Customs House and the Appraiser Building. Each of the subjects had their own camera. The agent notified contract guards inside the Appraiser Building. When the agent and guards went outside to contact the subjects, the three individuals hid their cameras and departed the area, with each subject traveling in a separate direction. The Baltimore City Police Department Intelligence Unit was notified, and the matter has been referred to an FPS Special Agent for further investigation. (ICE Daily Summary, 29 Dec 04; HSOC 4962-04)[90]

The January 5, 2005 brief also mentioned an incident involving a named Israeli citizen:

ISRAEL: Citizen of Israel Subject of TIPOFF and TSA No Fly has Visa Revoked on January 3. According to BTS reporting on 5 January, Samuel COHEN (DOB: 07/20/1969) arrived at LAX on COPA airlines from Lima, Peru, seeking admission as a

---

[90] Homeland Security, Homeland Security Operations Center, Homeland Security Operations Morning Brief, 30 December 2004.

131

visitor for pleasure. At LAX, the CT Watch determined that COHEN was a TIPOFF and NO FLY match. Close coordination resulted in the Department of State (DOS) revoking COHEN's visa on the spot. As a result of this revocation, COHEN was found to not be in possession of proper documents and was processed for an Expedited Removal. He is scheduled to depart 5 January, from the United States on COPA airlines flight CM303. (BTS Daily Operations Report, 5 Jan 05, HSOC 0033-05)[91]

On July 27, 2005, it was revealed that New York's Metropolitan Transportation (MTA) Authority's Interagency Counter Terrorism Task Force was maintaining a database of individuals stopped and questioned for filming bridge and tunnel crossings around New York City. Some of the people in the database were stopped on more than one occasion for filming and photographing bridges and tunnels and in one case an individual who was stopped for filming a New York area bridge was discovered to be driving the same vehicle as another person who was stopped earlier for filming the Verrazano-Narrows Bridge. An MTA source revealed that much of the filming did not involve regular tourists, but much more. The source said the filming "appear[ed] to be more than just casual filming." The filmers and photographers were concentrating on bridge beams (as in the case of the Memphis I-40 Bridge) and security checkpoints. The MTA database includes individuals stopped for filming the bridges and tunnels under the control of the MTA: Verrazano,

[91] Homeland Security, Homeland Security Operations Center, Homeland Security Operations Morning Brief, 5 January 2004.

Triborough, Throgs Neck, Whitestone, Henry Hudson, Marine Parkway, Cross Bay Veterans Memorial, the Midtown Tunnel and the Battery Tunnel.[92] A number of Federal law enforcement authorities report that suspicious Israelis continue to be stopped around the nation photographing and filming sensitive facilities and infrastructures but are not charged and brought to trial.

In October 2004, a suspicious Israeli was detained by the Delaware County, Oklahoma Sheriff's Department. Two miles of State Highway 20, east of Jay, were closed down while an Oklahoma State Police Bomb squad searched the Israeli's car for "possible terrorist activities." As has been the modus operandi in such cases, the FBI from Tulsa questioned the Israeli, who could not produce either a passport or a visa, and released him after seven hours. The Israeli had an Arizona driver's license showing an address in Gentry, Arkansas. The FBI said they were familiar with the Israeli. Delaware County Undersheriff Dale Eberle did not disclose the Israeli's identity since he was never arrested. The 40-year old Israeli, who was married to a U.S. citizen, had been traveling around the Tulsa area with a tubular camera on the roof of his car. Police were notified that the camera looked like a pipe bomb. Eberle said police were concerned that the Israeli may have been targeting the Pensacola Dam and two watersheds that feed Tulsa. The Israeli had recording devices and tools in his car, according to a police inventory. The Israeli had been asking questions about local industries in Jay and when

---

[92] Pete Donohue, "MTA has a secret film file," *New York Daily News*, July 27, 2005.

he stopped at a local diner he refused to use a glass or silverware because he did not want to leave fingerprints.[93]

On May 15, 2003, Cloudcroft, New Mexico Police Chief Gene Green stopped a U-Haul van in Cloudcroft, New Mexico, near the White Sands Missile Test Range, for speeding. According to the *Alamogordo Daily News*, the two truck drivers had Israeli driver's licenses and claimed they were hauling furniture from Austin to Chicago. Yet the rental agreement had expired two days earlier and New Mexico was way off track from the Austin to Chicago route. The Israelis then changed their story--they claimed they were dropping off furniture in Deming, New Mexico. But they could not provide a delivery address in the town. Also, their rental agreement was only for intrastate use in Illinois. Inside the truck, Chief Green found junk furniture not worth moving anywhere and 50 boxes that the Israelis claimed were a "private delivery." The Israelis were turned over to INS and nothing more was heard about them or their "cargo."[94] Consumers who have hired them have complained about suspicious behavior and illegal practices of Israeli-owned moving companies from Wisconsin to Florida to Pennsylvania. Advanced Moving Systems of Sunrise, Florida, an Israeli-owned moving company, complained that police in Pennsylvania, Wisconsin, and North Carolina

---

[93] Sheila K. Stogsdill, "FBI familiar with mysterious traveler," *The Daily Oklahoman*, October 5, 2004, p. 6A.
[94] Michael Shinabery, "New Mexico Police Stop Israelis with Suspicious Cargo," *Alamagordo Daily* News, May 19, 2003.

stopped several of its crews. The firm's owner, Zion Rokah, claimed the police were "xenophobic and racist."[95]

Almost one year earlier, on May 7, 2002, two Israelis were arrested in Oak Harbor, Washington, near Naval Air Station Whidbey Island. Police and Naval law enforcement investigators found traces of TNT and plastic explosives in a rental truck driven by the Israelis after they were stopped for speeding. One of the Israelis had an expired visa, an international driver's license, and no identification. They claimed they had delivered furniture in Oak Harbor and were on their way back to Canada. A bomb-sniffing dog reacted to traces of explosive material on the truck's steering wheel and gear shift. The FBI later said the explosive tests were negative and the INS, in keeping with tradition, refused to comment on the case.[96] In the days following September 11, a number of residents of Island County called emergency centers to report sightings of "Middle Eastern" looking men driving Canadian trucks.[97]

In a similar incident on May 21, 2004, two Israeli men, Tamir D. Sason and Daniel Levy, both of Metar, Israel, and reported to have been working for an Atlanta moving company, attempted to enter the King's Bay, Georgia U.S. Naval Submarine base. They were supposedly contracted to move someone from the base. As

---

[95] Mitch Lipka, "Rogue movers increasingly rip off consumers," *Philadelphia Inquirer*, February 1, 2003.
[96] Mike Barber, "Case of Whidbey Island 'terrorists' is a dud, FBI says," *Seattle Post-Intelligencer*, May 14, 2002.
[97] Ibid.

with the Whidbey Island incident, a bomb-sniffing dog alerted to a briefcase in the truck. Security guards became suspicious when one of the Israelis could not provide proper identification. The base went into a three-hour security lockdown and a bomb squad inspected the truck. As in the other cases involving Israelis trying to penetrate security perimeters, the Israelis were handed over to immigration authorities and the FBI refused comment. In addition to the FBI, the Georgia Bureau of Investigation and Navy Criminal Investigate Service were called in to investigate the Israeli incident.[98] King's Bay is close to Sea Island, Georgia, the site of the June 2004 G-8 Summit, a fact that obviously piqued the interest of law enforcement officials in the area.

On May 10, 2004, two other Israeli "movers" were apprehended suspiciously close to the Oak Ridge National Laboratories in Tennessee and the Federal Correctional Institution in Butner, North Carolina where convicted Israeli spy Jonathan Pollard was incarcerated. Driving a Ryder rental truck leased in Plantation, Florida, Shmuel Dahan and Almaliach Naor, led Unicoi County Sheriff Kent Harris on a high-speed chase. The Israelis claimed they were delivering furniture to West Virginia but Harris wondered why they would have been on the more remote two-lane U.S. Highway 23 rather than the faster Interstate 26. The Israelis also possessed false identification documents, Dahan a bogus Florida driver's license issued in Plantation, Florida and Naor a fake

[98] News4Jax.com, "King's Bay Naval Base Locked Down," May 21, 2004; Associated Press, "Suspicious Moving Van Prompt King's Bay Shutdown," May 23, 2004.

identification card. Harris also searched a storage facility the Israelis rented in Mars Hill, North Carolina. The FBI was called in to investigate but in typical fashion they turned the matter over the U.S. immigration officers who scheduled a deportation hearing. An FBI spokesman said the Israelis were guilty of nothing more than littering. Agents of the Bureau of Alcohol, Tobacco, and Firearms also joined the investigation. While chasing the Israelis, Harris noticed they threw a vial out of the truck. The Israelis later denied they threw anything out of the truck. The ejected container was reported to have contained a suspicious "fuel source" that was sent to the Tennessee Emergency Management office in Sevierville, Tennessee. It was later discovered to have contained a mixture of a cleaning fluid called Astromid 18, Gluconic acid, and water. Harris said he was not sure why the substances were mixed together. The Israelis also had a "Learn to Fly" brochure in their truck. Harris said he "got a sick feeling" when he saw the brochure and the business card of a Fort Lauderdale, Florida-based flight instructor named Nissan Giat, another Israeli citizen. Police feared the Israelis might have been targeting the Nuclear Fuel Services plant in nearby Erwin, Tennessee. A lawyer for the Israelis later claimed they meant no harm, that Naor possessed a fake identification card so he could get into a Miami nightclub. Naor's age was never given.[99] Although the Federal government said the Israelis

---

[99] Associated Press, "Israeli men arrested after high-speed chase in Unicoi County," May 10, 2004; Julie Ball, "Contents of Vial Linked to Israelis Not a Threat," *Asheville Citizen-Times*, May 12, 2004.

posed no danger, the state of Tennessee kept the case open. The DEA report on the activities of Israeli "art students" cited a case in which the Federal Protective Service arrested two Israeli art students in Plantation, Florida for possession of fake Social Security cards. Plantation was also the base of operations for Dahan.

On October 17, 2001, three Israelis driving a truck were discovered by Plymouth, Pennsylvania police with possession of a close-up videotape of the Sears Tower in Chicago. Plymouth Police Chief David McCann reviewed the tape and then found the Sony camera inside the truck. The police had responded to a call that the Israelis were illegally dumping furniture into a dumpster behind a Pizzeria Uno restaurant from a tractor-trailer truck registered in Florida. When the restaurant manager confronted the Israeli driver he drove off quickly from the scene. The leader of the team who drove the truck sporting the sign "Moving Systems Incorporated" was Moshe Elmakias. Two other Israelis, a woman named Ayelet Reisler, and a man named Ron Katar, were also questioned by Plymouth police after the truck was seen parked. Reisler had a German passport in one name and a prescription in another name. Whitpain, Pennsylvania Police later discovered that the truck's operator log had been falsified. All the evidence of the Whitpain and Plymouth police was collected by the FBI, which then deep-sixed the investigation in typical FBI fashion when it came to Israeli surveillance and espionage activity in the United States. Elmakias and Katar were turned over to the INS but Reisler was released.[100]

---

[100] Michelle Mowad, "2 found with video of Sears Tower,"

The Interstate 40 Hernando De Soto Bridge in Memphis was also an apparent surveillance target for the Israelis. According to the Arkansas State Police, a few days after 911, the FBI and Memphis police were alerted to two Israelis (officially reported to be of "Middle Eastern" appearance) taking photographs of the De Soto span and the older Interstate 55 Bridge. The Israelis were particularly interested in the undersides of the bridges. They had seven cameras of different sizes and makes. Upon being detained by the FBI, the men claimed to have diplomatic immunity and one produced a diplomatic passport. After the Israelis were turned over to the INS, the FBI dropped any further investigation.[101]

The Hernando de Soto Bridge in Memphis. Surveilled by Israelis a few days after 9/11

The Mercury, October 17, 2001.
[101] Confidential information.

In early October 2001, the FBI was on a nationwide search for six Israelis stopped by the police in the Midwest and found to be in possession of box cutters and "other equipment." The Israelis also had photos and descriptions of a Florida nuclear power plant and the Trans-Alaska Pipeline. The Israelis were traveling in groups of three in two white sedans. Although the INS ordered the men released, the FBI was reported to be furious that the Israelis were allowed to flee, possibly to Canada. The INS refused to reveal in what state the Israelis were stopped. Although their Israeli passports were reported valid, there was no way to know if their true identities matched those in the passports. The FBI refused to release the names and descriptions of the Israelis. FBI Director Robert Mueller and Attorney General John Ashcroft held a news conference on October 2, 2001 warning that a new wave of terrorist attacks could be expected in the United States. Their warning came after the Israelis were stopped in the Midwest.[102] In what may have been a related case, six Israelis were arrested in Cleveland in mid-October and were held incommunicado. A seventh Israeli woman was also reported to have been arrested.[103]

National Security Agency insiders revealed that NSA warned its employees against any interaction with proprietors of kiosks at the

---

[102] Martin Merzer, Curtis Morgan, and Lenny Savino, "Wanted By FBI: Still More Suspicious Men With Israeli Passports, Box-Cutters, Oil Pipeline And Nuclear Power Plant Plans," *Miami Herald*, October 3, 2001.
[103] Jim Galloway, "Israelis trapped in terror roundups cause worry at home, anger at U.S.," *Atlanta Journal-Constitution*, November 18, 2001, p. 15A.

Columbia Mall, a shopping center close to the NSA main campus in Fort Meade, Maryland. NSA apparently learned that the kiosk proprietors, who operate vending stalls for toys, body piercings, and jewelry, are connected to Israeli intelligence. The Israelis attempt to strike up conversations with NSA personnel to ascertain their jobs at the agency and attempt to create ongoing relationships.

The NSA warnings are similar to those issued by NSA in the mid-1980s when the author worked at the agency. Employees were routinely warned to avoid the bar at the Holiday Inn in Greenbelt, Maryland, which was determined to be a known hangout for Soviet KGB agents.[104]

Reporting on the activities of Israeli mall kiosks landed one Australian in jail. In 2009, in Perth, Australia, an Australian investigator was arrested and charged with violation of an Australian hate crime law for exposing the activities of Israeli-run mall kiosks owned by an Israeli firm in Melbourne whose products are called "Seacret - Minerals From The Dead Sea." The president of the Australian Union of Jewish Students lodged a criminal complaint against the investigator who maintained that Israeli nationals were attempting to obtain classified information on the Royal Australian Navy's Collins class submarine as well as other defense programs.

Information on naval forces appeared to be a high priority for the Israeli mall vendors. Cells of young Israeli intelligence operatives openly

[104] October 31, 2007, "NSA warns against kiosks at Columbia Mall in Maryland," WayneMadsenReport.com

141

solicited relationships with U.S. naval personnel in Norfolk from shopping mall kiosks, according to an informed source. It was learned that one such kiosk operated at the MacArthur Center Mall in Norfolk, Virginia where a number of U.S. Navy personnel from the nearby naval bases were regularly confronted by aggressive young Israelis selling Dead Sea cosmetic products who inquired about where the personnel were stationed and the nature of their jobs. Young Israeli women working at the kiosk also appeared to want to strike up a closer relationship with some of the male naval personnel.[105]

Israeli kiosk vendors were also aggressively seeking information at Washington, DC area malls. A number of young Israeli kiosk vendors working at, variably two to four kiosks, at the St. Charles Towne Center in Waldorf, Maryland inquired as to the work of passing shoppers, including a number of Air Force personnel who work at nearby Andrews Air Force Base and Navy personnel at the National Maritime Intelligence Center in Suitland, Maryland.[106]

Andrews Air Force Base is where Air Force One is home based.

On October 1, 2010, ABC Channel 4 in Salt Lake City led its news with this report by reporter Brent Hunsaker: "These salespeople say they're Israeli students . . . They even produce

---

[105] June 17, 2009, "Mossad still stalking malls near U.S. military bases," WayneMadsenReport.com

[106] July 24-26, 2009, "Israeli mall vendors story on WMR generates widespread interest," WayneMadsenReport.com

Israeli passports. They say they're selling their own artwork to raise money to open a gallery. So why would the Israeli art students want to know about the National Security Agency?" It turns out the Israelis were trying to find out about the newly-built NSA metadata center in Bluffdale, Utah.

On March 5, 2002, WJLA ABC 7 Washington, DC reporter Dale Solly led off with a similar news report about the activities of Israeli art students suspected of espionage prior to 9/11. On April 27, 2002, Solly, 53, was found dead in his Silver Spring, Maryland home just prior to him heading to the studio to go on the air. The county coroner ruled the death a heart attack.

Chapter 8 -- Coordinated global Mossad operations and bogus passports

On October 10, 2001, two Israelis, one a former Israeli Army Colonel and the other a Mossad agent, were arrested in the Mexican Congress with 9mm pistols and dynamite. According to the Mexican Justice Department official web site "the head of Congressional Security Salvador Alarcón verified that the Israelis had in their possession nine hand grenades, sticks of dynamite, detonators, wiring and two 9mm 'Glock' automatics." The Israelis were subsequently released after the intervention of the Israeli embassy in Mexico City.[107]

In 1990, the head of Colombia's secret police, General Miguel Maza Marquez, blamed Israeli paramilitary training for a wave of terrorist attacks in Colombia during the entire year. These included the bombing of an Avianca passenger jet in November 1989 that killed 117 people, assassinations of local political leaders, and two attempts on his own life. A bombing of Maza's police headquarters killed 63 people. Colombia responded to the Israeli involvement with terrorism by abrogating a 1962 no visa travel agreement with Israel.[108]

---

[107] "La PGR Informa Sobre La Situación De Los Sujetos Detenidos En La Cámara De Diputados," Justice Department of Mexico, October 12, 2001.
< http://www.pgr.gob.mx/cmsocial/bol01/oct/b69701.html>;
Ernesto Cienfuegas, "Army general and head of the PGR releases two Israelis arrested with guns and explosives inside the Mexican Congress," *La Voz de Aztlan*, October 15, 2001.

        In April 2004, New Zealand's Foreign
Minister called in Israel's ambassador to that
nation to complain about two suspected Mossad
agents arrested at Auckland airport after trying to
obtain false New Zealand passports. The
Australian Security Intelligence Organization
(ASIO) and the New Zealand Security Intelligence
Service (NZSIS) had cooperated in the sting of the
Israelis, identified as Elisha Cara and Uri Zoshe
Kelman. New Zealand and Australian police and
intelligence services tied the Israelis to the
Russian-Israeli mafia. Police were looking for a
third suspected Mossad spy, Zev William Barkan,
who was believed to have fled New Zealand for
Israel, and a fourth unidentified Israeli believed to
have gone into hiding in New Zealand. Barkan
was later discovered to have served at Israeli
embassies in Austria and Belgium. Police later
identified a New Zealander named Anthony David
Resnick, a 13-year veteran of the Israeli Defense
Force and a member of Auckland's Jewish
Council, as another conspirator in the Mossad
operation. Resnick reportedly fled to Israel. Cara
and Kelman were both released on bail with the
provision that they remain at two separate
Auckland hotels but both Israelis violated their
bail and checked out of their hotels.[109] They were
eventually sentenced to six months in jail and New
Zealand protested the illegal Mossad operation in

[108] Knut Royce, Peter Eisner, and Timothy M. Phelps,
"Gacha Got Assault Rifles from Israel; Weapons sold to
Antigua found at drug lord's home," *Newsday*, May 23,
1990, p. 4.
[109] Fran O'Sullivan and Bridget Carter, "Government
demands Israel return any bogus passports," *New Zealand
Herald*, April 19, 2004.

New Zealand by suspending relations with Israel.[110] There were reports that the Israeli operation extended to Australia and that the Australian Security Intelligence Organization (ASIO) may have tipped off its New Zealand counterpart about the espionage ring. After tipping off New Zealand about Cara and his accomplices, Australian agents raided Cara's rental home on Sydney's north shore. Cara's front was a Haifa-based travel agency called Eastward Bound.[111] After it was discovered that Kelman, an Israeli-Canadian, used a Canadian passport to enter New Zealand, Canada lodged a protest with Israel. In 1997, after two Mossad agents on an assassination mission were caught in Jordan using Canadian passports, Israel agreed to refrain from using Canadian passports in its intelligence operations.[112]

In February 2005, it was reported that Australia's Department of Foreign Affairs and Trade ordered a senior Israeli embassy officer in Canberra to leave the country for his intelligence ties to Cara and Kelman. Although the opposition Australian Labor and Green parties demanded details of the expulsion of the suspected Mossad agent, the John Howard government remained tight lipped about the matter.[113] Israeli President

[110] Yossi Melman, "NZ: 2 more passport suspects may have fled to Israel," *Ha'aretz*, July 25, 2004
< http://www.haaretz.com/hasen/spages/455480.html>
[111] Francis Till, "Fourth 'Israeli Spy' a Kiwi Academic," *National Business Review* (New Zealand), July 24, 2004
<http://www.nbr.co.nz/home/column_article.asp?id=9690&cid=5&cname=Asia%20&%20Pacific>
[112] Yossi Melman, "Canada to probe use of its passport in New Zealand affair," *Ha'aretz*, August 1, 2004.
[113] "Aussies Tight-Lipped Over Israeli Diplomat's

Moshe Katsav cancelled a March 2005 trip to New Zealand over the affair but he visited Australia on schedule.

On January 12, 2000, Indian Central Bureau of Intelligence (CBI) agents arrested 11 Israelis disguised as Islamic preachers ("tabliqis") before they boarded a Bangladesh Biman Airlines flight from Calcutta to Dhaka. The 11 Israelis, reported at first to be Afghans who spent some time in Iran, were to attend an Islamic conference in Dhaka but the government of Bangladesh denied them a visa. They all had one-way tickets to Dhaka, something that triggered alarms in Bangladesh. CBI officials were surprised when they discovered the arrested Islamic preachers were actually Israelis from the West Bank. After the Israelis were arrested, Israel exerted enormous pressure on the Indians to release them and permit them to return to Tel Aviv. A CBI official said, "It appeared that they could be working for a sensitive organization in Israel and were on a mission to Bangladesh." It was suspected that the Israelis, who could have been Afghan Jews, may have been recruited by Mossad to penetrate Al Qaeda cells in Bangladesh.[114]

On January 11, 2000, India's Bureau of Civil Aviation Security (BCAS) issued a Top Secret circular (NO: ER/BCAS/PIC/CIRCULAR/99), regarding a possible hijacking attempt on a Bangladesh Biman

---

Departure," New Zealand Press Association, February 6, 2005.
[114] Subir Bhaumik, "Aborted Mission; Investigation: Did Mossad attempt to infiltrate Islamic radical outfits in South Asia?" *The Week* (India), February 6, 2000.
< http://www.the-week.com/20feb06/events2.htm>

aircraft in India. The circular was signed by India's regional civil aviation security chief at Calcutta Airport and copies were sent to other Indian agencies as well as to the Bangladesh Biman office in Calcutta. It was this alert that helped India and Bangladesh nab the 11 Israelis the following day.[115]

Israeli *agents provacateurs* continued to be arrested in far-flung corners of the world. On November 9, 2005, Russian-born Vatang Agrunov (aka Bhatang Agranouve, Dahtang Mik Agarunov, and Bathan Agranouve), a 26-year old Israeli national and resident of Tel Aviv, was arrested in Trinidad on suspicion that he was involved in July 11, August 10, September 10, and November 3, 2005 bombings in Port of Spain. The bombings injured 28 people.[116]

Agrunov was also caught with a stolen Trinidad and Tobago immigration visa extension stamp. The police said Agrunov, a veteran of the Israeli military, stole the stamp from the Immigration Department in Port of Spain. The Trinidad police believed Agrunov was going to falsify his passport to remain in the country illegally. The Israeli embassy in Caracas intervened in the Agrunov arrest as did, suspiciously, the FBI. There was evidence that the FBI arrived in Trinidad after the July blast to cover up for the Israelis.[117] Local police complained that the FBI presence was not required and Prime Minister Patrick Manning said he was

---

[115] Ibid.

[116]

[117] "Israeli man held in forest," *Newsday* (Trinidad and Tobago), November 5, 2005.

148

unaware that anyone had requested help from the FBI at the time. Agrunov was deported from Trinidad to Israel on November 15, 2005, after the Israeli Embassy in Caracas, Venezuela paid his TT$ 2,500 (US$ 416) bail bond.[118]

Originally, Trinidad and Tobago authorities, including the Trinidad Special Anti-Crime Unit, the Special Intelligence Unit, the Criminal Investigation Division, and the local Interpol representative, had reason to suspect, from intelligence reports, that Agrunov was a terrorist. Agrunov had traveled through Spain and other European countries before arriving in Trinidad from Venezuela. Before obvious Israeli pressure was exerted on Trinidad and Tobago, Magistrate Maureen Baboolal-Gafoor denied Agrunov bail, citing him as a flight risk.[119]

As was the case with Israeli "art students" and "movers" who were detained in the United States and Canada, Agrunov played dumb, first claiming he did not steal the immigration extension stamp. According to the *Trinidad and Tobago Express*, in typical broken English and proffering a sob story, Agrunov told police, "I just want to say I take the stamp and finish this story. I don't want to stay in this country any longer. I want to go home. I just want to finish this and go back to my country because my family does not know what happened to me."[120]

---

[118] Stephen Cummings, "Israeli jailed in Trinidad to be deported," *Caribbean Net News*, November 17, 2005.
[119] Denyse Renne, "Israeli detainee to go on hunger strike," *The Trinidad Guardian*, November 8, 2005; Agency Caribbean Press, "Israeli national arrested in Trinidad threatens to go on hunger strike," November 9, 2005.
[120] John C. K. Daly, Intelligence Watch, UPI, November 9,

The bombings in Trinidad were at first blamed on local Muslim activists. Israel's Foreign Ministry labeled as "strange" the reaction of Trinidadian authorities to the presence of a suspected Israeli terrorist in their nation.

***

The DEA-INS continued to have a "keen interest" in the activities of the Israeli art students. The DEA believed there may have been links between the Israeli espionage teams and trafficking in the drug Ecstasy. Although the Israelis denied any espionage activity in the United States, some of their supporters in the Bush administration have defended the art students claiming, "It is quite normal for young Israelites to travel around the world for one year after they complete their military service."

A March 8, 2002, an editorial in the *Albuquerque Journal* summed up the general angst and suspicion over the activities of the Israeli art students:

> When U.S. authorities suspect an organized team of spies is seeking to infiltrate sensitive federal office buildings and the homes of government employees, they should arrest and interrogate to get to the bottom of the plot. Instead, a draft report from the Drug Enforcement Administration reports that young Israelis posing as art students but suspected of espionage activities were merely deported.

2005.

DEA first said the youths' actions "may well be an organized intelligence-gathering activity." But immigration officials deported the suspicious Israelis, said to number in the dozens, for visa violations.

Perhaps the officials had forgotten the case of Jonathan Pollard, a civilian Navy intelligence officer who gave classified information to the Israelis. It was an operation that Israel eventually acknowledged was known and approved of in the highest reaches of the Israeli government. Pollard has served some 13 years of a life sentence.

The recent arrests were made in a number of major U.S. cities from California to Florida, amid public warnings from U.S. intelligence agencies about suspicious behavior by people posing as Israeli art students and "attempting to bypass facility security and enter federal buildings."

The United States owes no duty to Israel to ignore spying. Israel, it could be argued, should at least be grateful enough to the United States that it should be reluctant to try to steal secrets.[121]

Perhaps the espionage incident would have faded entirely had it not been for the fact that similar art students, with unbelievable alibis, were caught in 2003 by Canadian security police around the Houses of Parliament in Ottawa.

---

[121] "Don't Ignore Spy Ring," *Albuquerque Journal*, March 8, 2002, p. A14.

On September 12, 2003, nine Israeli art students were arrested by Canadian Immigration officers and Ottawa police on Lisgar Street, just a few blocks from Parliament Hill, the day after the second anniversary of the terrorist attacks on New York and Washington. The Canadian police were tipped off by the Canadian Security and Intelligence Service (CSIS) that the Israelis, who were reported selling paintings in downtown Ottawa, were possible Mossad agents. The Israeli embassy spokesman in Ottawa used the same sort of language used by his Washington, DC counterpart to brush aside the arrests as routine, "We don't know full details about what the paintings were but it was a completely commercial matter," said Ben Forer, the spokesman for the Israeli embassy.[122] The arrests followed similar arrests of Israeli art students in Calgary, Toronto, and Saskatoon, according to Canadian Immigration officials. Residents of the Ottawa suburban district of Centrepoint had complained about Israelis selling fake art in 2001. Canadian authorities issued exclusion orders for all nine Israelis arrested in Ottawa and ordered them deported. Residents of the Ottawa suburban district of Centrepoint had complained about Israelis selling fake art in 2001.

In August 2004, two ringleaders of an Israeli "art student" door-to-door sales scam, Guy Grinberg and Yukov Senior, were deported from Canada for operating an art sales ring in Alberta. The "art student" ring operated in Calgary,

[122] John Steinbachs and Andrew Seymour, "Nine Israelis Face Deportation; Spy Agency Suspects They May Be Foreign Agents," *Ottawa Sun*, September 19, 2003, p. 8.

Edmonton, and Red Deer. Eight others were rounded up with the art sales ringleaders. Three apparently escaped Canadian law enforcement arrest.[123] In neighboring Manitoba, twelve Israelis – six men and six women – were arrested in Winnipeg for selling the junk art.[124]

It is interesting to note the answers that some of the Israelis gave when they were questioned by the immigration court. Thanks to the Canadian Immigration and Refugee Board, transcripts of the hearings were made available and they permit the reader to have an inside view of how the Israeli art selling rings operated, both in Canada and the United States. Five transcripts were provided but two provide interesting details of the art selling rings. The Canadian immigration authorities did not believe most of the evasive explanations provided by the Israelis. The answers of the team leader, Roy Laniado, are extremely interesting, especially his discussion of his "boss," an unnamed individual who traveled from the United States to Canada. As a result of the secrecy surrounding the INS roundup of some 120 Israeli "art students" in the United States, Americans never had the opportunity to know the inside story of how the operation worked:

Minutes of a hearing

---

[123] Paul Cowan, op. cit., *Edmonton Sun*, August 8, 2004, p. 6.
[124] Holliday, op. cit., *Winnipeg Sun*, August 8, 2004.

The Minister of Citizenship and Immigration
Le ministre de la Citoyenneté et de l'Immigration

and / et

EINAV SOFER
AMIT YEHUDAI

September 17th, 2003, Ottawa

BY MEMBER:

- So, I'll state that my name is Pierre Turmel. I am a member of the Immigration Division. Today is September the 17th, 2003, and I've been asked to preside an admissibility hearing concerning Einav Sofer.

BY MEMBER (to persons concerned)

- I'm sorry maybe for the pronunciation of your name.
A. You pronounce it good.
- And Amit Yehudai.

Q. That is you?
A. Yeah.

Q. Okay. First, I'd like to know if you fully understand English?
A. Yes.

Q. Or if you'd like to have the assistance of a Hebrew interpreter?
A. We understand everything.
- You understand everything.

Q. What about you, Mr. Yehudai?
A. I understand.

154

-	Okay.
Q.	Now, do you consent to the holding of this hearing in the presence of one another? Would you like to have your hearing separately, or if you are in agreement to have your hearing at the same time than Mr. Yehudai?
A.	We agree.
Q.	It is okay?
A.	(Mr. Cole) Yeah.
-	Okay, then.

The person to my right is the Minister's counsel, Madame Sybill Powell.

Q.	Now, you have been told that a hearing was to take place today. Am I correct?
A.	(Ms. Sofer) Yes.
Q.	You've received the documents to that effect?
A.	Yes.
A.	Yes.
-	On that Notice to Appear for the hearing there is a mention to the effect that you may be represented by a lawyer.
A.	(Ms. Sofer) No, we don't want to be represented by a lawyer.
-	You talk for yourself.
A.	I don't want to be represented.
Q.	You don't want to have a lawyer?
A.	I'm sorry.
A.	(inaudible)
-	You don't want a lawyer too. Okay, if you change your mind, you just let me know, okay, and I will act accordingly, okay.

There's another person in this room who is Mr. Yehudai's girlfriend. She is here as an observer. I will only state that observers

155

cannot intervene in any way during the course of the hearing. Okay.

Now, I have received documents. You have copies of the same. I will file these documents into the record of the hearing. The referral under subsection 44(2) of the *Immigration and Refugee Protection Act*, dated the 15th of September 2003, at Ottawa, will form Exhibit C-1 into your respective file.

EXHIBIT C-1 - SUBSECTION 44(2) REFERRAL - SEPT. 15TH, 2003

And the other document, which is the report made under subsection 44(1), dated the 12th of September 2003, at Ottawa, will form Exhibit C-2.

EXHIBIT C-2 - SUBSECTION 44(1) REPORT - SEPT. 12TH, 2003

Q. Now, Ms. Sofer, you've read that report?
A. Yes.

Q. Do you fully understand its contents?
A. Yes.

Q. And what about you, Mr. Yehudai, have you read it in full?
A. (no verbal reply)
-   You're nodding your head in an affirmative way.
A. Yes.
-   But you have to speak up. Everything is being recorded.
A. Okay.
-   Okay.

Q. And do you fully understand the content of the report?
A. Yes, sir.

-       Yes.

        Now, I'll tell you what I'm here for, okay. I first have to determine if you have a right to enter and/or remain into Canada. This right is restricted to Canadian citizens and permanent residents of Canada. If you are not such a person, I will then have to look at the report made against you in order to determine if you have contravened any of the dispositions of the *Immigration Act*, and more precisely, the ones appearing on the report.

        If I find you have not, I'll say it and the inquiry will end there. However, if I find that you have contravened the dispositions of the *Immigration Act*, I'll have no other choice but to make an Exclusion Order in your cases. This will mean that you will have to leave the country, and you will be prohibited from coming back to this country for a certain period of time. I'll tell you at the end of the hearing depending on the breaches to the *Immigration Act* how long you'll be prohibited from coming back.

Q.   Okay, understood?
A.   (Mr. Yehudai) Yes, sir.

Q.   Following my explanations, are you still ready to proceed now...
A.   Yes.
A.   Yes.

Q.   ...without a lawyer?
A.   Yes.
A.   Yes.
-       Yes, okay.

BY MEMBER (to Minister's counsel)

157

Q. Madame Powell, do you wish to call these persons as witness?

A. Yes.

- Okay.

BY MEMBER (to person concerned)

Q. Ms. Sofer, would you please stand up and raise your right hand. Do you solemnly affirm that the evidence you are about to give shall be the truth, the whole truth, and nothing but the truth?

A. Yes, your honour.

- Thank you.

A. Can I sit?

- Yes.

Q. Do you solemnly affirm that the evidence you will give at this hearing will be the truth, the whole truth, and nothing but the truth?

A. Yes, sir.

- Thank you.

BY MEMBER (to Minister's counsel)

- Your witness.

Q. Who do you want to start with?

A. Ms. Sofer.

- Ms. Sofer.

BY MINISTER'S COUNSEL (to person concerned)

- Please state your full name for the record.

A. Einav Sofer. It's. E.I.N.A.V. the first name, and the last name is S.O.F.E.R.

Q. And do you have any other names?

A. No.

Q. What is your date of birth?

A.   The 26th of December 1976.

Q.   And where were you born?
A.   In Israel, Vesai (phonetic), the name of the town.

Q.   Okay, and what is your citizenship?
A.   Israeli.

Q.   Are you Canadian citizen?
A.   No.

Q.   Are you permanent resident of Canada?
A.   Am I?

Q.   Do you have any permanent residency in Canada?
A.   No.

Q.   When did you enter Canada?
A.   The 6th of August.

Q.   Where?
A.   Toronto.

Q.   What was your purpose for coming to Canada?
A.   Travel in the beginning, then to go to work.

Q.   What did you tell the Port of Entry you were going to do in Canada?
A.   That I came to visit.

Q.   Just to visit?
A.   Yes.
-      Okay.

BY MEMBER (to person concerned)

Q.   You did not reveal you were coming here to...
A.   No.

Q.   ...engage in employment?
A.   No.

Q.   Why not?
A.   Because in the beginning when I came I didn't thought that I'm going to work. I thought (inaudible) in Canada because I'm student and I came only for two months, and then I met one guy who told me about this law, and I went to work and I didn't thought from the beginning to come to work. Because I was working as my money. And then he told me about this, and I thought why not. I didn't check this.

Q.   Did not you know before coming here that you...
A.   Coming to work, no.

Q.   That there was, this activity going on in Canada...
A.   No, I heard about.
-       There is advertising being...
A.   In Israel.
-       ...being made in Israel, yes.
A.   I heard from people that came here. They told me. Now I don't need to change everything.

Q.   You had not seen that ad before?
A.   Because didn't thought about coming to work because I was working in (inaudible) Service in Israel while studying. And I thought to myself, okay, this is too much, I'm going to come on vacation. I will come for two months, and then my boyfriend also will come to join me. And that's it. And then I heard about this here. I met one Israeli guy and he told me about this thing that they doing and I thought to myself why not. And it was a big mistake, excuse me.

160

Q.   And you intended on departing Canada at which date?

A.   With my boyfriend (inaudible).

Q.   When were you originally scheduled to depart Canada?

A.   We're supposed to be on 20 October, on the 20 of October because I'm starting my school on 26th.

-      Okay.

A.   So, my (inaudible). So until the end of summer vacation.

-      Okay.

BY MINISTER'S COUNSEL (to person concerned)

Q.   Who is, there's a note left Shara.

A.   Shahaman (phonetic), this is the Israeli guy that I met.

Q.   Okay, when did you meet him?

A.   In a bar. He told me about this thing.

Q.   Why did you come to Ottawa?

A.   Because I started in Montreal and... No, I started in Toronto, and then I went to Montreal, and then to Ottawa, and I thought to go after that maybe to Vancouver and to keep on travelling. And also to go after that to North. I can tell you, to see the Northern Lights in Alberta, in Saskatchewan. Just travelling in the big city in the beginning.

Q.   Did you know anybody in Ottawa?

A.   No, nobody. I didn't know anybody when I came to Canada actually. I know this family here, a family.

Q.   Who's Dan?

A.   Dan?

161

-        There's note that you spent two weeks in Montreal at a friend's house, Dan.

A.   Ah, this is a friend from Israel that I spent with there. I was staying with Isabel house, in Isabel house, and also with my friend Dan. But he's a guy I met also on the street. I didn't know him from Israel. Like, you know, Israeli people we always know one each other. If you go on the street and you just start to speak with people and that's it.

-        All right.

Q.   Now, when did you start to work in Ottawa?

A.   I don't remember the correct date.

-        Approximately.

A.   Around two weeks ago, something like that.

Q.   And what did you do?

A.   Like it's written.

BY MEMBER (to person concerned)

Q.   I'm sorry?

A.   Like it's written, selling (inaudible).

-        Okay.

BY MINISTER'S COUNSEL (to person concerned)

Q.   And how many did you sell?

A.   I don't know exactly how much. But I can tell you how much I believe around, like around eight-hundred (800), six-hundred (600).

Q.   Eight-hundred (800) dollars in total or per week?

A.   No, per week.

162

Q.   Did you have an employment
     authorization?
A.   No.

Q.   Did you apply for an employment
     authorization?
A.   No.

BY MEMBER (to person concerned)

Q.   So you were making between six-hundred
     (600) and eight-hundred (800) dollars a
     week?
A.   Yeah.

Q.   You were doing good?
A.   (inaudible).
-    You were doing good.
A.   Yes.
-    You're a good saleswoman.
A.   Actually I didn't do it for the selling, but it
     was important.

Q.   I'm sorry?
A.   I didn't do it for the selling because I
     thought about something else. I didn't do
     it for the money actually.
-    No, no, yeah, yeah.

Q.   But I mean it was easy for you to sell those
     paintings?
A.   Yes, because I can explain about art, and I
     know a lot about art because I'm offering
     art in Israel my country. So (inaudible),
     and like I said in the beginning my main
     idea wasn't to sell them. My main idea
     was to come to people and talk to them
     about the thing that I know, to give them
     maybe a small knowledge about art, what
     I'm doing. And (inaudible) because this.

BY MINISTER'S COUNSEL (to person
concerned)

163

Q. Were these your paintings?

A. No, no. I'm doing my own painting in
Israel. I'm doing my own art.

BY MINISTER'S COUNSEL (to member)

- Those are all the questions I have for her.

A. Okay.

BY MINISTER'S COUNSEL (to person
concerned)

- Now, sir, could you please state your name
for the record.

A. My name is Amit Yehudai,
Y.E.H.U.D.A.I.

Q. Okay. You have any other names?

A. No.

Q. So what is your date of birth?

A. Sixth of August 78.

Q. Sixth of August?

A. Seventy-eight.

- Okay.

Q. So where were you born?

A. In (inaudible).

Q. What is your citizenship?

A. Israeli.

Q. Are you a Canadian citizen?

A. No.

Q. Are you permanent resident of Canada?

A. No.

Q. When did you enter Canada?

A. Fifth of August.

164

Q. Where?
A. Toronto.

Q. And what did you tell the Port of Entry
your purpose of coming to Canada was?
A. For visiting.

Q. And what was your purpose of coming to
Canada?
A. My purpose was to see (inaudible)

Q. Had you met before?
A. Yes.

BY MEMBER (to person concerned)

Q. Where?
A. In Toronto.

Q. You've been here before?
A. (no verbal reply)

Q. When was that?
A. Probably two years ago.

Q. Two years ago?
A. (no verbal reply)

Q. Have you kept in touch over the past two
years?
A. (no verbal reply)

BY PERSON CONCERNED-MS. SOFER (to
member)

- Sir, (...inaudible...)
A. Yeah.
- I'm sorry.

BY MEMBER (to person concerned)

Q. Do you know each other?

165

A.   (Ms. Sofer) (inaudible).

Q.   You've travelled together?
A.   No.

Q.   You arrive on the same day?
A.   Yes. We met in the airport, sir.
-       Okay.
A.   And then (inaudible).
-       Okay.

BY MINISTER'S COUNSEL (to person
concerned-Mr. Yehudai)

Q.   Who met you at the airport?
A.   Who met me, Roy.

BY MEMBER (to person concerned)

Q.   I'm sorry?

BY MINISTER'S COUNSEL (to person
concerned)

Q.   Roy?

BY MEMBER (to person concerned)

Q.   You met Roy Maniato?
A.   Yes.

Q.   At the airport. You knew him?
A.   I knew him from Israel but in another
        situation.

Q.   Why was he at the airport to meet you on
        arrival?
A.   No, he was just picking me up and then I
        went to Montreal.

BY MINISTER'S COUNSEL (to person
concerned)

166

Q.   Did he take you to Montreal?
A.   What?

Q.   Did he take you to Montreal?
A.   No, I rented a car.

Q.   How long did you stay in Montreal?

A.   Like one month, something like that.

BY MEMBER (to person concerned-Ms. Sofer)

Q.   Have you also got picked up at the airport
      by Roy Maniato?
A.   No. I went, I took a taxi because I didn't
      know where. I took a taxi to hotel, and
      then Amit came to the hotel, and that I
      arrived, (inaudible). And then it was after
      I came with him to Montreal.

Q.   With Roy?
A.   No, with Amit. Because I didn't know
      (inaudible).

BY MINISTER'S COUNSEL (to person
concerned-Mr. Yehudai)

Q.   So Roy picked you up at the airport and
      you went back to his house?
A.   No, to hotel.

Q.   To his hotel?
A.   Not this hotel. I look (...inaudible...) hotel
      next to the airport.
A.   (Ms. Sofer) I can, if (inaudible) to talk, or
      you can check also on the ticket. I can and
      I went, nobody came to pick me. I took a
      cab to one place that my friend that she
      was travelling, she told me to go in
      Toronto. That it's a very good place and a
      cheap one. And then Amit also came to
      this place. And then the day after we went
      together to Montreal.

167

Q.   So you just met in the airport, or you met at the hotel?

BY MEMBER (to person concerned-Ms. Sofer)

Q.   At the hotel, not at the airport?
A.   Yes, at the airport.

BY MINISTER'S COUNSEL (to person concerned-Ms. Sofer)

Q.   So you just went to Montreal then?
A.   Yeah, because, you know, I didn't know anybody, so he said that he was going to Montreal, so I went.

BY MINISTER'S COUNSEL (to person concerned-Mr. Yehudai)

Q.   All right, so you went to Montreal and visited your girlfriend?
A.   Yes, my girlfriend.

Q.   And that was your reason for coming to Canada?
A.   Yes.

Q.   What was your... why did Roy pick you up? Did you contact him before you were coming to Canada?
A.   It was like, like it you said about the advertisement, something there in advertisement. So it was like kind of, like an option, like an (inaudible).

Q.   Okay, so you had answered the ad in Israel?
A.   What?

Q.   You called the ad in Israel?
A.   Yes, yes. I just want, you know, it was like my summer vacation, I like to

168

travelling, so I called them to say an option. Maybe it could, you know. This could be just an option.

Q.   And when did you find out Roy was involved?

A.   I didn't know that Roy. They told me like okay, if you want, you can come, some guy named Roy will wait for you. That's it.

BY MEMBER (to person concerned)

Q.   The person you talked to told you...

A.   No...

Q.   ...told you could come and a person by the name of Roy ...

A.   Will pick me up, exactly.

Q.   ...will pick you up...

A.   Exactly.

Q.   ...at the airport?

A.   Exactly, because this kind of service they offer.

-    Yeah.

A.   Like small (inaudible) for you like when you come.

-    Uh-hum.

A.   But then the first and the main reason I came (...inaudible...) and I told him I go to Montreal and I need to think about it like this, to see if I want to go.

BY MINISTER'S COUNSEL (to person concerned)

Q.   But he was picking you up, but you knew that a person that you had contacted about work was picking you up at the airport?

A.   He pick me up.

-    Okay.

169

Q.   So at the Port of Entry did you mention
        that you were going to be meeting with a
        future employer?

A.   He wasn't my employer. I met him also in
        Israel. He was my friend. I didn't know.
        They told me Roy, but I knew him from
        Israel two years ago. When I talked with
        him...

Q.   When you knew that they told you that
        someone from their work would pick you
        up at the airport and meet you, is that
        correct?

A.   Yes.

Q.   Okay, and his name was Roy?

A.   Yes.

-       You didn't know you knew him before.
        This is somebody named Roy that picked
        you up at the airport and he was involved
        in selling paintings, okay.

A.   This is true.

Q.   So when you came to the airport and the
        Port of Entry person said why are you
        here, you said?

A.   For visiting.

-       Okay.

A.   But I want to explain something. When he
        picked me up I wasn't like in a status of a
        (inaudible). I told him also in the
        beginning that I come for Canada for my
        reason, and if it's like, if I can combine go
        with him then it's okay. But my reason
        coming was to see the (inaudible). So
        when he picked me up, it wasn't like he
        picked up to work. He picked me up like
        this service, like this company like it's
        doing like a favour for you. They can
        (inaudible) you want to do. They treat you
        nice. So, you know, it's like kind of
        (inaudible).

170

Q.   How much did you make selling
       paintings?

A.   Like six-hundred (600), seven-hundred
       (700).

BY MEMBER (to person concerned)

Q.   When did you start selling paintings?
A.   What?

Q.   When did you start selling paintings?
A.   I sell frames not paintings.

Q.   I'm sorry?
A.   I sell frames not paintings.

Q.   When did you start selling frames?
A.   After like (...inaudible...)

Q.   How long after you had arrived?
A.   Like three weeks and a half, something
       like that.

Q.   And in which city have you sold those
       frames?
A.   In Ottawa.

Q.   Here only, not in Montreal?
A.   Not in Montreal.

BY MINISTER'S COUNSEL (to person
concerned)

Q.   When did you meet up with Roy again?
A.   After I had no contact with him, and I
       came Toronto.

Q.   Did you have an employment
       authorization?
A.   (inaudible).

171

Q.   Did you ever apply for employment
       authorization?
A.   (inaudible).

Q.   Pardon?
A.   No.

BY MINISTER'S COUNSEL (to member)

-      I have no further questions.
A.   Thank you.

BY MEMBER (to person concerned)

Q.   Mr. Yehudai, ...
A.   Yes.

Q.   ...where is your girlfriend living?
A.   My girlfriend?
-      Yes.
A.   In Montreal.

Q.   Where? What's her address?

A.   It's Rue Cuvillier.

Q.   I'm sorry?
A.   Rue Cuvillier.
-      Would you spell that out for me.
A.   I don't know the spelling in French. It's
       Rue Avenue East Cauvillier, it's
       C.A.U.V.I.L.L.E.R. Rue Cauviller it's near
       Sherbrooke.
-      Okay, she is in the back of the room, I'll
       ask her.

BY OBSERVER (to member)

-      La rue Cuvillier.
A.   Cuvillier.

BY MEMBER (to person concerned)

172

Q.   Okay, is she living alone there or with her parents or?
A.   No, she live alone.
-    Alone.

Q.   Is she employed, would you know?
A.   Yes.

Q.   What does she do for a living?
A.   She work in a bookstore, in a bookstore.

Q.   In a bookstore?
A.   Yes.

Q.   Is full-time employer?
A.   I don't know what is the status, but I think so.

Q.   Was she working five days a week?
A.   Five days, yes, four or five days.
-    Four, five days a week, okay.

Q.   And was she working during the time you were at her place?
A.   Yes.

Q.   She was?
A.   ...

Q.   She didn't take any holidays?
A.   She had sometimes like three days off so we could be together. But otherwise when she's working she work like from ten to six or nine to ten. So still we have the day.
-    Uh-hum.
A.   And sometimes I go to meet her at her work (inaudible).

Q.   I'm sorry?
A.   Sometimes I go to meet her at her work and (inaudible). So then (inaudible).
-    Yeah, okay.

173

Q.   And when you came to Ottawa in order to engage in employment did she come to Ottawa with you?

A.   If she come with me?

-      Yeah.

A.   No, I go on the weekends to Montreal.

Q.   In a weekend, during the weekend?

A.   Yes.

-      Yeah, okay.

BY MEMBER (to Minister's counsel)

-      Madame Powell, I'd like to hear you with regards to the misrepresentation allegation concerning both of them.

A.   Of what Ms. Sofer has told us...

Q.   I'm sorry?

A.   From what Ms. Sofer...

-      Yes.

A.   ...has told us today...

-      Yes.

A.   ...she basically says that she came to Canada and within a few short hours met up with someone. They both went to Montreal the next day. A few weeks later they end up in Ottawa not knowing that they would end up in Ottawa, I don't believe, together. She says that she knew nothing about this, about this painting before she came to Canada. She met somebody on the street who told her about it. And yet she would have been driving in a car the day after she arrived with someone that was very knowledgeable about it all the way to Montreal.

I find that what she said today that she came to travel, and that she just basically meet people on the street and move in with them. Difficult to believe in 2004, and I

174

don't believe that her only purpose to come to Canada was to solely travel and would like to see her described as misrepresentation, as well as (inaudible).

In terms of...
- Hold on a second. I'll give her immediately an opportunity to respond.

BY MEMBER (to person concerned)

Q. You've heard what Madame Powell said?
A. What can I do now? I did something wrong. I know that I did something wrong. In the end the most important thing that I did something wrong. The most important thing if I would say that I come to visit, nobody would believe me because everybody is looking on the last thing, the last thing was very terrible, is very wrong. And I can understand why she find it hard to believe me. I can understand her and I respect what she's saying because it sound to her very strange and she don't know how the Israeli people like us how we talk to one each other. When we see one people in the street and just start talking one to each other. So, but the main important thing is that I did something wrong and I know it.
- Okay.

BY MEMBER (to Minister's counsel)

- As concerns Mr. Yehudai.
A. Mr. Yehudai had contacted this company before he left Israel. He had agreed to have someone from the company pick him up at the airport. Someone who he says that he later found out he already knew and someone that was very involved in the painting business. I find it difficult to believe that he didn't have at least some

175

plan to take part in working when he came. And I believe that although it may not have been his main reason, certainly it was part of... part of what he planned to do here, and I believe that he should be described for misrepresentation (inaudible).

BY MEMBER (to person concerned)

- Yes.
A. Regarding what she say, quite agree with, you know, just want to say it again that like she said the main reason come was not for work. I didn't talk before about the work. It was only like an option, possibility. Because I'm a student. And then the thing that they pick me up, you know, it's like to save the twenty-five bucks for the taxi, which for me it's not worth it. And that's it till I come to Montreal. I'm not saying after I work, and (inaudible). That's it.

- Ms. Sofer and Mr. Yehudai, you have both testified during the course of the admissibility hearing. Your testimony, firstly, permits me to conclude that you have no right to enter and/or remain into Canada given that you are not Canadian citizens nor permanent residents of Canada. You both are citizens of Israel by birth in that country.

You have both testified having arrived in Canada on the 5th of August 2003, at Toronto. And you have both subsequently engaged in employment without having first obtained the written authorization from the Immigration Department. You were selling paintings, and frames for you, Mr. Yehudai, and received a commission as a remuneration. You earned just

176

between six to eight-hundred dollars per week.

So obviously there's an allegation that has been established in that you contravened the dispositions of paragraph 41(a) of the *Immigration and Refugee Protection Act* in that on a balance of probabilities there are reasons to believe you are a foreign national who is inadmissible for failure to comply with a requirement of the *Act*. That was the requirement of obtaining a written authorization before engaging in employment.

Now, there was another allegation in both cases to the effect that you would also be inadmissible into Canada by reason of having exercised, whether directly or indirectly, a misrepresentation relating to a relevant matter which induced or could have induced in error in the administration of the *Act*.

Now, you have testified, Ms. Sofer, that you had no clue of this working activity before reaching Canada. That you have learned about this once in Canada, and then decided to engage in employment. But I'll come back on your testimony at a later time during the course of this decision. I want first to turn to Mr. Yehudai who said that prior to his coming to Canada he had seen an ad in a newspaper and contacted a person. He was explained what the work was all about and has agreed to meet a person at the airport on the day of his arrival. So a representative of the company was there by the name of Roy, but it happened that he was someone he already knew for some years. He didn't know at first that Roy

177

would have been the person he knew for some years.

So, I do not know if I'm going to believe that part of his testimony. But if I were to believe it, what I realize is that Mr. Yehudai contacted the company, inquired about what was involved as a work, agreed to be met the very day of his arrival in Canada. And notwithstanding the fact he is trying to convince me that the only reason for his coming to Canada was to pay a visit to his girlfriend. His girlfriend lives in Montreal and three weeks after his arrival he moves to Ottawa and engage in employment for that person called Roy who is acting as a supervisor, and his girlfriend stays in Montreal where she is fully employed and had no holidays but is returning every weekend to see her. So I would say that we might be playing on words here, Mr. Yehudai, when you say that the main reason for your coming to this country was to see your girlfriend.

Well, I may use the same tactic here. It might have been true that the major reason for your coming was to see your girlfriend, but there was a secondary and a complementary reason to your coming, which was to make money during your stay by working in Canada. Otherwise you would not have prior to departing Israel contacted the company in order to see what involved the work you could perform while visiting Canada. So I believe in all likelihood that you had the intention, even it is true to say you were coming here first to see your girlfriend at the same time you had the intention of engaging in employment which you have not revealed. So I find the second allegation has been established.

178

Now, as concerns Ms. Sofer, there are very strange coincidences in that she arrives here on the same day that Mr. Yehudai, though on a different flight, and she happens to meet also Mr. Roy because she met Yehudai at the hotel where she went. And quite curiously it is the same hotel where Roy brought Yehudai when he picked him up at the airport. And you happen to travel to Montreal together, and you happen to be now working both of you for the same Roy.

So I think I can conclude on a balance of probabilities, I might be wrong, but I'm looking at the odds, and when examining all these facts, I conclude on a balance that your coming into Canada was not only to do tourism, but while doing tourism, work at the same time to maybe make some bit of money to help your tourist visit. So I find this allegation to have been also established.

So I'm ordering in both of your cases exclusions from Canada, and you are prohibited from coming back to this country for a period of two years. If you want to come back to Canada within that two year period, you first present yourself to a Canadian Embassy and ask for the written consent of the Immigration Minister. So a Canadian visa officer will examine the reasons why you want to come back here, and if he finds you have valid reasons for coming back and you are acting out of good faith, then you'll be issued the special consent.

A.   (Ms. Sofer) Just a question, sir.
-     Yes, you can.

179

A.   Maybe you can give me two years and Amit only one year because, sir, maybe we don't know but it's the law, you know.

-     No, no, no, that is the law. That is two years for each of you. I cannot give you one of his years.

A.   Why not, sir?

-     No, no, I can't. That's how it goes.

Today's hearing is now terminated.

Minutes of a hearing

The Minister of Citizenship and Immigration
Le ministre de la Citoyenneté et de l'Immigration

and / et

ROY LANIADO

September 17, 2003, Ottawa
<u>BY MEMBER</u>:

-     Good Morning. My name is Pierre Turmel. I am a member of the Immigration Division. Today is September 17, 2003, and I've been asked to preside an admissibility hearing concerning Roy Laniado.

<u>BY MEMBER</u> (to person concerned)

Q.   That is you?
A.   Yes, sir.

Q.   Mr. Laniado, I understand you are fluent in English. You did not have the services of a Hebrew interpreter?

A.   No, I don't.
-     No. Okay.
     The lady to my right is the Minister's counsel, Madame Sybill Powell.

Q.   Now, Mr. Laniado, I guess you have been told that an admissibility hearing was to take place today. Am I correct?
A.   Yes, sir.
-     On the Notice to Appear for this hearing, which you received, there's a mention to the effect that you have the right, if you want, to retain the services of a lawyer. It is a right that you have. It is not an obligation as you may choose to proceed on your own.

Q.   So what do you want to do today?
A.   I think I can explain myself in most of the case.

-     Good. I till then proceed. However, if any time during the course of the hearing you change your mind and you feel that the presence of a lawyer would become necessary, all you have to do is let me know. Okay.
A.   I have a question.
-     Yes.

A.   After the hearing conclude,...
-     Yes.
A.   ...could then I come to a lawyer and appeal upon this hearing?
-     No, there's no appeal.
A.   No appeal.
-     There's no appeal.
A.   Okay.
-     That there be a lawyer here or not, there won't be any appeal against the outcome of the hearing.
A.   Okay.
-     Okay.

181

Now, you have a package of documents. I have the originals here. The very one is a referral for inquiry under subsection 44(2) of the *Immigration and Refugee Protection Act*. This document was made at Ottawa, on the 15th of September 2003. This document only gives me jurisdiction to proceed with the hearing. I will file it as Exhibit C-1.

EXHIBIT C-1 - SUBSECTION 44(2) REFERRAL-SEPT. 15, 2003

The other document which is most important to you is the report made under subsection 44 sub (1) of the *Immigration and Refugee Protection Act*. It is also dated, well, it is dated the 12th of September 2003.

Q.   Have you read that report in full?
A.   I read it briefly. Now I go...

Q.   You want to have a couple of minutes?
A.   Sure.
-     There are two pages. While you're reading I'll say that I will file this report as Exhibit C-2.

EXHIBIT C-2-SUBSECTION 44(1) REPORT-SEPT. 12TH, 2003

A.   There is one thing that is not copy right.
-     Okay, do not explain immediately. You will be given an opportunity during the course of the hearing to testify, okay.

Q.   Now, you've read it in full. Now, do you understand what it says in there?

A.   Yes, I do.

182

	Okay. Let me give you a bit of explanations as to the purpose of the hearing and its possible consequences for you. First of all, I'm here to determine if you have a right to remain into Canada. Canadian citizens and permanent residents of Canada have a right to stay here. If you are not such a person, I will then have to look at the well-foundedness of the allegations appearing on the report. And if I find these allegations to be true, I'll have no other choice but to make an Exclusion Order in your case. This is a removal order. This will mean that you will have to leave Canada, and you will also be prohibited from coming back to his country for a certain period of time.

If I were to find that the first allegation, the only first allegation is founded, you'll be prohibited from coming back to Canada for one year. If I find that both are, that is the last one too, then you'll be prohibited for two years. If you ever want to come back here within that period of time, you will firstly have to present yourself to a Canadian Consulate or Embassy in any country where Canada has official representatives, and this in order to ask for and obtain the Minister's written consent.

Q.   Are those explanations clear to you?
A.   Yes.
-      Okay.

Q.   Following my explanations, are you still ready to proceed on your own?
A.   Yes, sir.

-      Okay. Now, the Minister's counsel, Madame Powell, has the burden of proof. She will most likely call you as a witness. She may call other witnesses. She may

183

present documentary evidence. On your
side, you'll have the opportunity to
examine all the evidence, cross-examine
witnesses, if any persons are being called
to testify.

A.   Okay.

-     And at your turn, you'll be given an
opportunity to present your own evidence.
Okay.

A.   Yes, sir.

BY MEMBER (to Minister's counsel)

-     Madame Powell.

A.   Yes, Mr. Member.

Q.   You wish to call him as a witness?

A.   Yes, please.

BY MEMBER (to person concerned)

-     Mr. Laniado, you're being called as a
witness to this hearing. I'd like you to
please stand up and raise your right hand.

Q.   Do you solemnly affirm that the evidence
you are about to give shall be the truth, the
whole truth, and nothing but the truth?

A.   Yes, sir.

-     Thank you. Have a seat.

BY MEMBER (to Minister's counsel)

-     Your witness.

BY MINISTER'S COUNSEL (to person
concerned)

-     Please state your full name for the record.

A.   Mr. Roy Ezra Laniado.

Q.   Any other names?

A.   No.

184

Q. What is your date of birth?
A. February 7, 1979.

Q. And where were you born?
A. Israel.

Q. What is your citizenship?
A. Israeli.

Q. Are you a Canadian citizen?
A. No.

Q. Are you permanent resident of Canada?
A. No.

Q. When did you enter Canada?
A. March 23rd.

BY MEMBER (to person concerned)

Q. Of which year?
A. 2003.

BY MINISTER'S COUNSEL (to person
concerned)

Q. And where was that?
A. Toronto.

Q. When you came to Canada what did you
tell the Port of Entry officer what's your
reason for coming?
A. Travelling.

BY MEMBER (to person concerned)

Q. I'm sorry?
A. I told him I'm coming to travel.

Q. As a tourist?
A. Yes.

185

Q.   Why were you coming to Canada?
A.   To travel.

Q.   Was that your sole reason for coming to
Canada?
A.   Yes.

Q.   On the 12th of September you were
arrested with a number of others. Can you
tell me why you were with this group of
people?
A.   Yes, I came here to meet the guys.

BY MEMBER (to person concerned)

Q.   You came here to meet who?
A.   To meet the persons that were arrested.
-      With you, okay.
A.   To give them frames, paintings. To leave
the same day to Toronto.

BY MINISTER'S COUNSEL (to person
concerned)

Q.   Why were you giving them frames and
paintings?
A.   For them to sell them.

Q.   Was that the first day you met them?
A.   No.

Q.   How often had you supplied them with
frames and paintings?
A.   Once a week, once in two weeks.

Q.   Did you charge them for these frames and
paintings?
A.   I wouldn't charge them in advance, no.

BY MEMBER (to person concerned)

Q.   You would not charge them in advance,
     but would they have to pay you back?
A.   Yes, after they sold them, they would have
     to pay, to pass me the, yes.

BY MINISTER'S COUNSEL (to person
concerned)

Q.   How much would they give you like per
     painting, or was there a set amount each
     week they had to give you, or?
A.   They were amount to be give me for the
     painting, 80 dollars painting, and 85
     dollars frame.

Q.   How long were you doing this? How many
     weeks?
A.   Approximately between 16 to 18 weeks.

Q.   How many weeks after coming to Canada
     would that have been?
A.   Eight weeks.

BY MEMBER (to person concerned)

Q.   You started eight weeks after having
     entered Canada?
A.   Yes.

BY MINISTER'S COUNSEL (to person
concerned)

Q.   How did you get this job?
A.   There was a ad in the newspaper in Israel.

Q.   When was that?
A.   The beginning of March.

Q.   Before you came to Canada?
A.   Yes.

187

Q.   So you had the job before you came to
       Canada?
A.   Yes. But it was just an option for me. I
       came here originally to travel. And then
       because of my lack of cash, a lot of
       money, I started working. I was supposed
       to work for a period of time and then to
       continue my travelling. To leave Canada
       to South America.

BY MEMBER (to person concerned)

Q.   Okay, how much are you getting for
       yourself out of these ...
A.   This money?
-      Yeah.
A.   I would get eventually between two to
       three and half thousand dollars a month.
       Like I get it every...

Q.   That's for your own?
A.   That's for myself, yes.
-      Okay.

BY MINISTER'S COUNSEL (to person
concerned)

Q.   The people that worked for you how much
       did they get?
A.   It's something you won't be able to say
       because some of them they don't sell
       anything, so they wouldn't get anything.
       Some of them sold a few I cannot really
       say.

Q.   Did they get a percentage of the profits per
       painting?
A.   From their sales, yeah.

Q.   Did you have any expenses...
A.   Yes.

Q.   ...other than... what were your expenses?

188

A.   Cell phone, vehicle, accommodation.

Q.   Accommodation for yourself...
A.   Yes.

Q.   ...or accommodation for them?
A.   For myself.

Q.   Cell phone, you said cell phone.
A.   Cell phone.
-    Car.
A.   Car and accommodation, vehicle and obviously fuel. I'm driving a rental. It's not my vehicle. Everything just to support myself.

Q.   Who made their room?
A.   They did.

Q.   They paid their room?
A.   I paid it in advance and they returned me the money. They couldn't afford a month in advance.

Q.   So you paid a month in advance?
A.   Yes.

Q.   All right, so...
A.   It's not came, it didn't came from my pocket, but yes.

BY MEMBER (to person concerned)

Q.   Where did it come from?

BY MINISTER'S COUNSEL (to person concerned)

Q.   Where did the money come from?
A.   Like I explained the officers from immigration, I'm not in charge of this business. I'm not the head of this group of students. There was another guy, there is

189

actually another guy or two or twenty, I don't know what. The one that I'm aware of on top of me. I would take the money from them and I had to, give him the money after I got my share. And from this money I could rent their houses, and then when they return me, I would add this to the sum and give it to him.

BY MEMBER (to person concerned)

Q. Who is that person?
A. (inaudible) I don't have any specific information on him. You must understand it's the owners of this kind of business wouldn't like to expose themself into any...
-   Okay.
A. Any problem with the law. So it's usually they stay, like in the case, they stay in the dark, no names, no phone numbers, no address.
-   Well...
A. Even if I wanted to...
-   ...you have to get in touch with him. You have to return the money.
A. He would have called me to my cell phone, let me know when can I meet him in Toronto. Most of the time in Toronto. He would give me the money and...Excuse me, I give him the money.
-   Yes.
A. He give me the frames and the paintings. So.

Q. Does that person lives in Canada? Would you know if that person is a Canadian citizen or a foreigner, or?
A. He's an Israeli.
-   Yeah.
A. He told me he lives in the States. I wouldn't take his word of.
-   Yeah.

190

<u>BY MINISTER'S COUNSEL</u> (to person concerned)

Q.   Why were you hired as the group leader of this group?

A.   He liked me I guess in some sort of way. I met with him in Israel and I spoke with him for a while and he...

<u>BY MEMBER</u> (to person concerned)

Q.   You met with him in Israel prior to coming to Canada?

A.   Yes. The way I got into this job is through his help. I called him and I got the message they will come to me if I (inaudible) the job. I met him at (inaudible).

-    Yes.

A.   He explained to me, first of all, I was supposed to call him as if I would work as a salesman going door to door trying to sell the paintings. Then he asked me about my military service. What I did here, what did I did there. And my military service, has a certain...

-    Background.

A.   ...experience, background. It was sufficient for this kind of job. That's why eventually he wanted me to do this job and not other. Want to be salesman or something else just...

-    Be a kind of a supervisor.

A.   Yes. And I must say that at least for the concern of taking care of the employees after you found out they're not Musad [sic] agents and I hope that it's clear for everyone.

Q.   That?

191

A.   We're not Musad [sic] agents. That they
        were taken care of very good. I took care
        for everything they needed starting
        accommodation, going onto all sorts of
        problems they had, all sorts of issues they
        needed to solve as foreigners in a country.
        And they were treated in the most decent
        way I could manage.
-       Uh-hum.

BY MINISTER'S COUNSEL (to person
concerned)

Q.   How much money did you bring to
        Canada with you?
A.   I came with me with four-thousand U.S.
        dollars and a very big ...not a lot of
        Canadian dollars. But when I met my, my
        parents were already in Canada last week
        actually, so they brought me another sum
        of Canadian.

Q.   How much money did you have when you
        were arrested?
A.   First of all, I never got a report from the
        police on how much money did they
        seized us.

Q.   How much do you think was there?
A.   There was three-thousand and four-
        hundred or five-hundred U.S. dollars, and
        between seven to eight thousand in
        Canadian dollars.

Q.   How did you have four-thousand dollars
        U.S. to come to Canada? Were you
        working in Israel?
A.   First of all, I used to work, not in the last
        year, but I lived and worked in Israel. I've
        been working since I was 16.

BY MEMBER (to person concerned)

192

Q.	But how long have you been out of employment?
A.	Two years, two years and something.

Q.	Out of employment prior to your coming here?
A.	But I, once again I was working since I was 16.
-	Yes.
A.	Providing myself.
-	Yes.
A.	And I didn't let... I do have a wealthy family that has put some money aside. So this state of my life when I do mostly travelling I'm using this money to travel.
-	Okay.

<u>BY MINISTER'S COUNSEL</u> (to person concerned)

Q.	Where have you travelled?
A.	Oh, no.

Q.	No, no, but where?

<u>BY MEMBER</u> (to Minister's counsel)

-	Well, Madame...

<u>BY MEMBER</u> (to person concerned)

-	Sir, do not answer the question.

<u>BY MEMBER</u> (to Minister's counsel)

-	That question is not real...
A.	Relevant.
-	...relevant to the allegation.
A.	All right.

<u>BY MINISTER'S COUNSEL</u> (to person concerned)

Q. How long had this group been in Ottawa?
    Not all members of the group but this
    group of sales people.
A. Approximately a month and a half.

Q. Did you have a work permit, an
    employment authorization to do this work?
A. No.

Q. Where did you travel in Canada?
A. All over. East coast, West coast, all over.

Q. Did you know anybody in Canada?
A. Yes.

BY MINISTER'S COUNSEL (to member)

-   That's all my questions.
A. Thank you.

BY MEMBER (to person concerned)
-   Madame Powell, has ended her
    presentation of evidence, and she believes
    that your testimony is sufficient to
    establish the well-foundedness of the
    allegations brought against you.

Q. Is there anything you would like to add on
    your side?
A. I don't have any question, but I have a few
    things to say if your honour is willing to
    hear it.
-   Go ahead.
A. I would like to say first of all that I really
    appreciate and love your country. I think
    it's one of the greatest country in the world
    if you look at it, and I travelled a great, a
    lot. I travelled a lot so I can tell the
    difference between a state to another.
    Since I started working with this here I had
    a lot of ideas and lot of thoughts about
    opening here a business in Canada. I do
    not want to get a Canadian citizenship. I

194

would like to spend the rest of my life in Israel. I'm satisfied with my citizen, my Israeli citizenship and yet I think that Canada has a lot to offer to foreign investors. And I think that me with my, if I can say, talent and my will to work, I can help Canada a lot.

\- But this, Mr. Laniado, you'll have to do through the proper channels.

A. I know. That's...

\- That is you'll have to file for permanent residency...

A. A week in advance.

\- ...at an embassy.

A. A week in advance to the incident, to the arrest, actually I started doing some, going to lawyer and this and that to try and open a business. Legal business, to stop doing the monkey business stuff, and to open it legally to pay taxes like everyone else and do everything right, on the right way. I'm aware that what I have done is wrong and I can see why the Canadian government is doing us this hearing and eventually will probably send us to our main land.

\- Yes.

A. I would like to at least have the opportunity to say that I would like some day to come back to Canada, and on a legal permit, of course, to open a business and to try and do something which I know can be very nice here. Can help me, can help Canada, can help the people of Canada. Because after all Canada is a growing country and you need both young men to work here, or women. And I would like to add something else that is relative to this case, if I can.

\- Yeah.

A. That when we got arrested, so eventually when we set off to our homes, (inaudible) so some of our belongings wasn't returned

195

to us. I had a wallet, a leather wallet, 35 dollars inside the wallet with two credit cards, two debit cards, an Israeli Driving License, my International Driving License.

Q.   Those documents were seized by the cops, by the policemen?

A.   They weren't seized. They were, I have downstairs you can, over here maybe you can see photographs of all these documents. But somehow they weren't returned to me. I came here, we were released on Friday evening. Saturday, Sunday I came here there was no one here. There was no one to talk to. I left messages.
-       Okay, okay.
A.   Impossible. And right now nobody finds it by the way.

Q.   Oh, the documents are lost?
A.   The documents are here, but my credit cards, my Driving License, I don't have any four or five...

Q.   Where are those documents? Do you have them on file?
A.   The police and the immigration blame each other for losing them. Basically it's...
-       Well...
A.   Right now when you seize all the money.
-       Yeah.
A.   And all my documents and my passport is here, in Canada I'm stuck.
-       Unfortunately, I cannot intervene in this matter, but I understand your concerns and you will certainly have to inquire before immigration and the policeman in order to find out what happened to those cards. And someone will have to certainly answer and give reasons why those cards

196

have suddenly disappeared. That's all I can say on this.

A.   I'm not saying for anything other than reason that right now I don't have any ID. I can...

-     No, ...

A.   Because my family...

-     ...immigration has seized your passport. The passport will be returned to you when you will leave Canada.

A.   But the thing that until then I don't have anything. A few days ago I was pulled over by a cop. It took almost three hours until, like for a traffic violation.

-     Yes.

A.   ...it took two hours until he finally understood who I am, what am I doing here, and what can he do to me or whatever. He could arrest me immediately if he wanted. He was just nice trying to solve this thing in a good way. I don't have any credit cards, so I need to make new ones. I cannot do it. I don't have any ID. I don't have any money. I cannot get any Western Union money transfers. And please get me my passport back. I'm not asking you to find the wallet, but any kind of ID. I'm not gonna run from Canada with anything. I have bond of fifteen-thousand dollars.

-     Yes, Mr. Laniado, this will have to be discussed with immigration. I cannot order immigration to return you the passport. They're the only ones who are to decide on whether they will keep it on their file or they will return it to you. Okay. But I'm sure Madame Powell is taking good notes of what you're saying at this time, and I hope immigration or the policemen will be able to trace your credit cards and the rest of your belongings.

A.   Thank you, sir.

197

	Mr. Laniado, the evidence adduced during the course of today's admissibility hearing consisted of your sole testimony which reveals at first that you are a citizen of Israel by birth in that country on February 7th, 1979. You are not a Canadian citizen nor a permanent resident of Canada, and this is sufficient for me to conclude that you have no right to remain into country.

Now, you testified having entered Canada, on March 23rd, 2003, at Toronto. At that time you said, you told the examining immigration office at the Port of Entry that you were coming here as a tourist. You also said during the course of today's admissibility hearing that this was, as a matter of fact, the sole reason for you coming to Canada. You said it was the sole reason for your coming to Canada when the question was asked of you.

A. Ah, to travel.

- Yeah.

A. Ah, yes.

- Now, you got arrested on the 12th of September 2003, and you have now admitted that you've been working in Canada as a supervisor. You're getting between two to three, or thirty-five-hundred a month, plus you have expenses that are being paid. That is your cell phone, accommodation, vehicles, fuel and all that kind of things. You never asked for nor obtained a working authorization.

You said that prior to your coming to Canada, you had seen ad in a newspaper in Israel and you called someone, met you in Tel Aviv and discussed what the work was all about. And because of your qualifications, it was determined that you would not act as a salesman door to door

198

but you would rather supervise a team of salesmen. And you started working eight weeks after your arrival in Canada.

Having fully considered the evidence before me, I find, Mr. Laniado, that you are a person described in Paragraph 41(1)a) of the *Immigration and Refugee Protection Act* in that, on the balance of probabilities, there are grounds to believe you are a foreign national who is inadmissible for failing to comply with the *Act* through an act or an omission which contravenes directly or indirectly a provision of the *Act*, and that is the requirement of Section 30 sub (1) which states that you cannot work in Canada unless authorized to do so under the *Act*.

Now, there was another allegation to the effect that, on a balance of probabilities, you would be inadmissible for misrepresentation of a material fact. You said that when examined at the Port of Entry you told the immigration officer you were coming here in order to sightsee the country. And you answered Madame Powell's question by saying that this was the only reason why you had come here. However, when considering that prior to initiating your trip to Canada, you contacted someone who had put an ad in a newspaper about work in Canada. So to inquire about the details of that job, you even met with the person who, following discussions, has offered you to be a supervisor rather than selling paintings door to door. So I think in all likelihood you weren't only coming here to sightsee Canada, but you were coming here so to engage in employment as well. Maybe doing both at the same time. But you also had the intention of engaging in employment since you had already... you have already discussions prior to your coming to Canada about this kind of job.

So I find that the second allegation is also established on a balance of probabilities, and consequently I am hereby making an Exclusion Order against you. And this will mean that you will be removed from Canada. You will be called to leave, and you will be prohibited from coming back to Canada for two years.

A.   For two years.

-       For two years you can't come back. If you want to come back though, you may come back within that two year period of time, but you need to obtain the Canadian Immigration Minister's written consent which could be obtained any Canadian Embassy in any country where Canada has a delegation.

A.   In how much time should I leave?

-       This immigration will tell you how long they'll give you to make arrangements and leave the country. Okay.

Today's hearing is now terminated. I'll have you sign the order.

The transcripts of the deportation hearings of the art students are revealing. Former and well-educated former members of the Israeli military acted as if they never knew it was against the law to work in another country without a permit. There were references to an unnamed "boss" who lived in the United States and owners of the art selling operation who wanted to avoid run-ins with law enforcement. Perhaps the art students in Canada were merely unaware but couple the Canadian art operation with the American operation carried out just two years prior and a pattern of deception emerges. The motto of the Mossad is noteworthy when pointing to its foreign operations: "By way of deception, thou shalt do war."

There was an interesting postscript to the Israeli espionage activity in the United States before, during, and after 911. In December 2004, it was reported that a former senior U.S. government official, commenting on the FBI's raid of AIPAC's Washington offices, stated that in 2001 the FBI discovered a "massive" Israeli espionage operation on the East Coast, specifically including New York and New Jersey.[125] National Security Adviser Rice and her deputy Stephen Hadley were both briefed on the FBI investigation of Israeli espionage in the United States shortly after they took office in early 2001.[126] A Justice Department source confided that it was Attorney General John Ashcroft who personally ordered the investigation of the Israelis stopped in the months prior to 911 – a decision that proved fateful for the thousands of people who perished on September 11.

---

[125] Richard Sale, "FBI Steps Up AIPAC Probe," UPI, December 9, 2004.
[126] Richard H. Curtiss, "New Spy Investigation Suppressed at Crucial Juncture," *Washington Report on Middle East Affairs*, November 2004, pp. 26-27.

Chapter 9 -- More Israeli Smoking Guns"

A female Israeli "art student" who lived on an Israeli kibbutz for a year and who is also a British national, told a confidential source in London that in the weeks prior to 9/11 she was "selling art in Washington [DC]." Before her arrival in Washington, the Israeli art student said she was in the San Francisco Bay Area attending college as an "art student" but denied selling any art while there. She also said she spent some time in South Carolina prior to 9/11.

The leaked Drug Enforcement Administration (DEA) report on the activities of Israeli art students prior to 9/11 revealed that female Israeli art students were active in Palo Alto and Fresno. The British-Israeli art student said that on the morning of 9/11 she was standing outside the Pentagon. She admitted she never saw a plane hit the building but saw a huge "hole" in the building after an explosion. The art student also said that she was in Times Square in New York the next day, September 12, attending a memorial service for the 9/11 victims. She said she had a ticket to fly out of New York's John F. Kennedy Airport on September 12 but that because commercial planes were grounded she had to find another way to leave the country.

The art student said she 'had to get out' of the United States because she did not have a proper visa to continue working in the country. She said she left the United States after crossing the Canadian border. When quizzed why she left so quickly after 9/11, the art student replied that she "had to leave cause the United States Government thought Israelis had something to do with 9/11."

The female art student later began operating two market kiosks in London that primarily sold women's hand bags. The kiosks were in Notting Hill and Camden in two neighborhoods where a number of people from Pakistan, Afghanistan, and Arab countries reside.

On December 31, 2008, two Israelis who worked in a hair products kiosk at the Rosengaard Mall in Odense, Denmark, on the island of Funen, were shot and slightly wounded by a Danish assailant who was born in Lebanon and was of Palestinian origin. One of the Israelis owned the kiosk, which sold Dead Sea hair and skin care products, a usual front for Israeli intelligence operations. Apparently, the Israelis' activities had caught the attention of certain Middle Eastern-born youth in Odense days before the shooting. The youth began harassing the two Israelis. The Danish Security and Intelligence Service was reported to have been notified about the incidents involving the Middle Eastern youth and Israelis by Odense police. The two Israelis, both in their 20s, had only been in Denmark for about a week.

Israeli charge d'affaires Dan Oryan said it was disturbing that the two Israelis were targeted merely because they were Israelis. Oryan's reaction was in keeping with other Israeli denials and obfuscation that their young nationals are engaged in intelligence operations while masquerading as art students, mall kiosk vendors, and moving company employees.

The National Security Agency and other U.S. intelligence agencies have warned that Israeli mall kiosks are suspected Israeli intelligence fronts. However, in bust after bust, the Immigration and Customs Enforcement (ICE) bureau of the Homeland Security Department under then-Secretary Michael Chertoff, merely deported Israelis who worked illegally on tourist visas. No Israelis were ever charged with espionage or other major crimes.

Israeli national Ohad Cohen entered the United States multiple times in 2004 to manage kiosks and supervise other Israelis, all working in the United States illegally, at Oakview Mall in Omaha and Gateway Westfield Mall in Lincoln, Nebraska. Nine Israelis were arrested and all were deported without a trial. Cohen was forced to forfeit over $35,000 he made from kiosk sales in Nebraska.

In December 2004, the FBI and ICE arrested 15 Israelis at various Minnesota mall kiosks for selling illegally copied software in electronic games. Yonatan Cohen was charged with illegal copyright violations. Also in 2004, ICE agents arrested three Israelis working at a mall kiosk in Grand Forks, North Dakota. Grand Forks and Omaha are home to major Air Force bases.

On October 31, 2001, nine Israelis were arrested by Immigration and Naturalization Service agents while working at a Toledo, Ohio area mall kiosk selling Israeli toy helicopters called "Zoom Copters." Seven Israelis were released but two, Yaniv Hani and Oren Behr, were deemed "special interest" cases in a federal law enforcement probe of terrorism activities and the 9/11 attack. Hani and Behr told the Associated Press that FBI agents asked them if they were spies for the Israeli government. FBI agents also asked the Israelis detailed questions about their Israeli military service.

Mark Regev, then a spokesperson for the Israeli embassy in Washington and later a shill for the government of Israel in Jerusalem, denied that any Israelis arrested in the United States were espionage agents.

After 9/11, some thirty Israelis were arrested in St. Louis, Kansas City, and Columbia, Missouri for being in the United States illegally. Other Israeli kiosk workers were detained in California. The Israelis said they were hired by a Miami Beach-based company called Quality Sales to work at shopping mall kiosks in Missouri.[127]

***

In 2011, British intelligence provided a "tip" as to what it knew about Mossad's involvement with 9/11.

It was learned that British intelligence prepared a report in February 2002 that stated the Mossad ran the Arab hijacker cells that were later blamed by the U.S. government's 9/11 Commission for carrying out the aerial attacks on the World Trade Center and Pentagon. Details of the British intelligence report were, according to British intelligence sources, suppressed by the government of then-Prime Minister Tony Blair.

---

[127] "Mossad's modus operandi exposed. From art students to kiosk operators," WayneMadsenReport.com, January 5, 2009.

However, a description of the report stated that a Mossad unit consisting of six Egyptian- and Yemeni-born Jews infiltrated "Al Qaeda" cells in Hamburg (the Atta-Mamoun Darkanzali cell), south Florida, and Sharjah in the United Arab Emirates in the months before 9/11. The Mossad not only infiltrated cells but began to run them and give them specific orders that would eventually culminate in their being on board four regularly-scheduled flights originating in Boston, Washington Dulles, and Newark, New Jersey on 9/11.

The Mossad infiltration team consisted of six Israelis, comprising two cells of three agents, who all received special training at a Mossad base in the Negev Desert in their future control and handling of the "Al Qaeda" cells. One Mossad cell traveled to Amsterdam whereby they submitted to the operational control of the Mossad's Europe Station, which operates from the El Al complex at Schiphol International Airport. The three-man Mossad unit then traveled to Hamburg where it made contact with Mohammed Atta, who believed they were sent by Osama Bin Laden. In fact, they were sent by Ephraim Halevy, the chief of Mossad.

The second three-man Mossad team flew to New York and then to southern Florida where they began to direct the "Al Qaeda" cells operating from Hollywood, Miami, Vero Beach, Delray Beach, and West Palm Beach. Israeli "art students," already under investigation by the Drug Enforcement Administration for casing the offices and homes of federal law enforcement officers, had been living among and conducting surveillance of the activities, including flight school training, of the future Arab "hijacker" cells, particularly in Hollywood and Vero Beach.

In August 2001, the first Mossad team flew with Atta and other Hamburg "Al Qaeda" members to Boston. Logan International Airport's security was contracted to Huntleigh USA, a firm owned by an Israeli airport security firm closely connected to Mossad -- International Consultants on Targeted Security - ICTS. ICTS's owners were politically connected to the Likud Party, particularly the Netanyahu faction and then-Jerusalem mayor and future Prime Minister Ehud Olmert. It was Olmert who personally interceded with New York Mayor Rudolph Giuliani to have released from prison five Urban Moving Systems employees, identified by the CIA and FBI agents as Mossad agents. The Israelis were the only suspects arrested anywhere in the United States on 9/11 who were thought to have been involved in the 9/11 attacks.

The two Mossad teams sent regular coded reports on the progress of the 9/11 operation to Tel Aviv via the Israeli embassy in Washington, DC. It was learned from a Pentagon source that leading Americans tied to the media effort to pin 9/11 on Arab hijackers, Osama Bin Laden, and the Taliban were present in the Israeli embassy on September 10, 2001, to coordinate their media blitz for the subsequent days and weeks following the attacks. It is more than likely that FBI counter-intelligence agents who conduct surveillance of the Israeli embassy have proof on the presence of the Americans present at the embassy on September

10. Some of the Americans were well-known to U.S. cable news television audiences.

In mid-August, the Mossad team running the Hamburg cell in Boston reported to Tel Aviv that the final plans for 9/11 were set. The Florida-based Mossad cell reported that the documented "presence" of the Arab cell members at Florida flight schools had been established.

The two Mossad cells studiously avoided any mention of the World Trade Center or targets in Washington, DC in their coded messages to Tel Aviv. Halevy covered his tracks by reporting to the CIA of a "general threat" by an attack by Arab terrorists on a nuclear plant somewhere on the East Coast of the United States. CIA director George Tenet dismissed the Halevy warning as "too non-specific." The FBI, under soon-to-be-departed director Louis Freeh, received the "non-specific" warning about an attack on a nuclear power plant and sent out the information in its routine bulletins to field agents but no high alert was ordered.

The lack of a paper trail pointing to "Al Qaeda" as the masterminds on 9/11, which could then be linked to Al Qaeda's Mossad handlers, threw off the FBI. On April 19, 2002, FBI director Robert Mueller, in a speech to San Francisco's Commonwealth Club, stated: "In our investigation, we have not uncovered a single piece of paper -- either here in the United States, or in the treasure trove of information that has turned up in Afghanistan and elsewhere -- that mentioned any aspect of the September 11 plot."[128]

---

[128] Eric Lichtblau and Josh Meyer, "Details of Sept. 11 Plot Elude U.S. Investigators," *Los Angeles Times*, April 30, 2002.

The two Mossad "Al Qaeda" infiltration and control teams had also helped set up safe houses for the quick exfiltration of Mossad agents from the United States.

Two El Al sources who worked for the Israeli airline at New York's John F. Kennedy airport confidentially related that on 9/11, hours after the Federal Aviation Administration (FAA) grounded all civilian domestic and international incoming and outgoing flights to and from the United States, a full El Al Boeing 747 took off from JFK bound for Tel Aviv's Ben Gurion International Airport. The two El Al employee sources were not Israeli nationals but legal immigrants from Ecuador who were working in the United States for the airline. The flight departed JFK at 4:11 pm and its departure was, according to the El Al sources, authorized by the direct intervention of the U.S. Department of Defense. U.S. military officials were on the scene at JFK and were personally involved with the airport and air traffic control authorities to clear the flight for take-off. According to the 9/11 Commission report, Transportation Secretary Norman Mineta ordered all civilian flights to be grounded at 9:45 am on September 11. British intelligence sources revealed that the six-man Mossad team was listed on the El Al flight manifest as El Al employees.

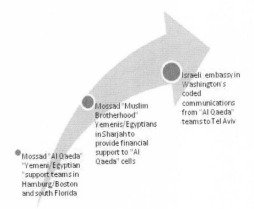

Israeli embassy in Washington's coded communications from "Al Qaeda" teams to Tel Aviv

Mossad "Muslim Brotherhood" Yemenis/Egyptians in Sharjah to provide financial support to "Al Qaeda" cells

Mossad "Al Qaeda" "Yemeni/Egyptian "support teams in Hamburg/Boston and south Florida

The Mossad sequence of events

On October 23, 2006, Yechezkel Wells, a 21-year old dual U.S.-Israeli citizen, pleaded guilty to phoning in a false bomb threat on August 26, 2006 to Long Beach (California) Airport Emergency Services from a pay phone. Wells claimed that he made the call because he was late for his flight and hoped to delay his plane from taking off. Wells said that there was a bomb on the Jet Blue flight from Long Beach to Fort Lauderdale, Florida. The Jet Blue flight was delayed for one hour.

Not much was known about Wells. He claimed he was a student but there is no information on what school he attended. The college was Talmudic University in Miami Beach. Wells pleaded guilty to a single felony count of conveying false information of a threat targeting an airplane. Wells faced a maximum of five years in prison or probation. In October 25, 2006, the author reported that if "past is prologue, we can expect the Bush administration to agree to probation in return for Wells's deportation to Israel, where he, like hundreds of other Mossad, Metsada, Shin Bet, Sayeret Matkal, and LAP agents caught engaged in false flag terrorist and psychological operations in the United States before, during, and after the 9/11 attacks, can continue to ply their trade in deception."

On January 29, Wells was sentenced in Los Angeles to probation but not deportation to Israel. Instead, U.S. District Court Judge Florence-Marie Cooper sentenced Wells to six months of home detention, where he would wear an electronic monitoring bracelet; a $1000 fine; 200 hours of community service; and two years of probation.

Wells was not acting alone in the bomb threat. An affidavit signed by FBI agent David Gates revealed that Wells and three friends were detained by FBI agents after the bomb threat but that the three friends were released after questioning. Wells's mother, Tziporah Wells, flew from Israel to attend the sentencing hearing. The *Los Angeles Times* reported that Ms. Wells put her fingers in her ears while Judge Cooper reprimanded Wells.

Wells had spun quite a tale to those he encountered. He told a Jet Blue counter employee at Long Beach that he had to get home for his brother's funeral in Miami the next day. When he was denied boarding because he was too late for check-in, he phoned in the bomb threat. His attorney, Donald Etra, said Wells was in Los Angeles to attend a wedding. The light sentence of

Wells was a result of the weak charges brought by Assistant U.S. Attorney Donald F. Gaffney.

Etra was a 1968 Yale graduate and classmate of George W. Bush and fellow member of the Skull and Bones, a director of Russell Trust Association (the holding company for the Skull and Bones), and was appointed by Bush to the U.S. Holocaust Memorial Council. Bush and First Lady Laura Bush attended Etras's wedding in 1985 and Etra and his family have been overnight guests at the White House. Etra donated to the Bush-Cheney 2000 campaign.

Compare Wells's lenient treatment to what became of Canadian citizen Maher Arar who was falsely arrested in 2002 by U.S. authorities in New York in transit through JFK Airport en route back to Canada from abroad. Innocent of the charges brought against him, Arar was sent to Syria where he was tortured for 10 months and forced to make false confessions. Canada has cleared Arar, apologized to him, and planned to make financial restitution. The U.S. still keeps Arar on no-fly and terrorist watch lists and has refused to apologize to him as Canada has demanded. Arar's only crime is that he was an Arab. Wells, on the other hand, escaped proper justice because he was an Israeli. [129]

An Israeli art student cased the offices of an investigator of the suspicious February 26, 2004, death of Macedonian President Boris Trajkovski. Trajkovski's Beechcraft King Air 200 crashed near Stolac, Croatia in southern

---

[129] January 31, 200, "Phone in a bomb threat to an airplane and get probation," WayneMadsenReport.com

Bosnia while en route to an investors' conference in Mostar.

After the crash, U.S. ambassador to Macedonia Lawrence Butler quickly met with Nikolai Gruevski, the Minister of Finance in the VMRO-DPMNE government.

Although Trajkovski, a Methodist minister, was also a member of the VMRO-DPMNE party he was viewed as less accommodating to international demands for privatization of state enterprises in Macedonia.

After Trajkovski and his party were killed in the plane crash, Macedonian and Bosnian authorities complained that NATO's investigation of the plane crash was secretive and the two countries aviation authorities were kept in the dark. Many Macedonian officials were opposed to allowing the United States to investigate the crash and there was confusion about who had access to the two "black boxes" on Trajkovski's plane. NATO troops stationed in Bosnia were the first to arrive at the crash scene.

In April 2004, Crvenkovski, the pro-American, won the Macedonian presidential election. VMRO-DPMNE officials charged that there was massive ballot box stuffing in th election and refused to accept the results.

Although the crash of the King Air 200 was blamed on dense fog, on February 27, 2004, the Xinhua news agency reported another scenario, one that suggests terrorism:

"A suspected **blast** occurred on board shortly before the crashed Macedonian presidential plane went lost from radar, a local Bulgarian radio reported Thursday. The report quoted Sasho Yordanovski, editor-in-chief of the Macedonian magazine *Forum*, as saying that there have been two versions of the cause of the tragic incident, which claimed the lives of the Macedonian president and other eight people. One version attributed the accident to bad weather conditions in the area early Thursday and the other suggested a technical failure of the 25-year-old aircraft . . . Besides the president, the victims include his councilors Dimka Ilkova-Boshkovic, Risto Blazhevski and Anita Lozanovska, foreign affairs official Mile Krastevski, two bodyguards Atse Bozhinovski and Borsi Velinov, and two pilots Marko Markovski and Branko Ivanovski."

The author learned that an independent firm hired to investigate the crash was not able to conduct its investigation because its private investigator received death threats if he went to the Balkans to conduct his probe. In addition, a young Israeli male "art student" showed up selling art sketches at the U.S. offices of the investigation firm. The Israeli arrogantly entered three office rooms in the facility without invitation. When asked by office workers what he was doing, he abruptly left. No other offices in the vicinity received a visit from the art student. It was later discovered that the office's surveillance camera had been disabled by an intruder.

The reported involvement of Israeli security advisers in the coup d'etat in Honduras also puts into another perspective the following report from the Drug Enforcement Administration (DEA) on the espionage activities involving Israeli art students in the months prior to 9/11:

"Tegucigalpa Country Office

170. On February 28, 2001, a couple attempted to sell at the residence of the Tegucigalpa Country Attaché. His neighbors advised the Country Attaché that a man and a woman in a red car were trying to open the CA's gate. The neighbors asked the couple what they wanted and advised them that no one was home. The couple left the area. No identification information was revealed."

Some FBI counter-intelligence agents are painfully aware that Israelis traveling on tourist visas in the United States and who mask their true intelligence functions as art students, movers, and mall kiosk vendors pose a significant hostile intelligence threat to U.S. national security. However, the FBI agents are also aware that any push to pursue Israeli agents will result in career-ending personnel actions taken as a result of pressure from the all-too-powerful Israel Lobby in the United States.[130]

On January 25, 2010, the U.S. State Department issued an in-depth report on the operations of Israeli kiosk vendors in shopping malls across the United States. Although the report, released in the tranche of cables exposed by WikiLeaks, did not mention the links of these Israeli vendors to Israeli intelligence operations in the United States, the report does provide an insight into the vendors' ties to money laundering, organized crime, and visa violations.

The U.S. embassy in Tel Aviv recommended a ban on U.S. visas for any Israeli having just completed military service. Most of the Israelis

---

[130] July 10-13, 2009, "Israeli art students show up at interesting times," WayneMadsenReport.com

operating in shopping malls recently completed their obligatory military service. But as numerous U.S. intelligence reports have stated on these vendors, many specialized in demolitions, signals intelligence, and counter-intelligence operations/

The kiosk vendors were also active in Canada, as cited in this CBC report from December 22, 2010:

"A man accused of bringing illegal workers to Halifax will be allowed to stay in Toronto until his next court appearance.

Iftash Jacob was released from custody Thursday after surrendering his passport and posting a $7,500 bond.

He must report to the Canada Border Services Agency every week and return to Halifax provincial court in February to enter a plea . . .

Jacob and nine others — all from Israel — were arrested Wednesday in a raid on a home in Halifax and kiosks at three shopping malls in the region.

Border Services officials arrested an 11th person on Thursday outside a courthouse.

Eight people — two women and six men — pleaded guilty Wednesday to working in Canada without authorization, and each was ordered to pay a $1,000 fine. They are allowed to stay in the country but not work here."[131]

---

[131] "Accused ringleader of illegal workers in court," CBC, December 22, 2010.

The State Department cable summary on the
suspicious Israeli kiosk vendors:

ID 10TELAVIV140
SUBJECT IN DEPTH: DEAD SEA COSMETICS
AND SKINCARE INDUSTRY
FRAUD
DATE 2010-01-25 00:00:00
CLASSIFICATION UNCLASSIFIED//FOR OFFICIAL
USE ONLY
ORIGIN Embassy Tel Aviv

1. (SBU) SUMMARY: Tel Aviv has been
investigating visa fraud in the U.S. Dead Sea
Cosmetics and skincare industry since 2007, when
it became a noticeable problem. From September
2008, Dead-Sea related fraud has been one of Tel
Aviv's Fraud Prevention Unit's (FPU) and
Assistant Regional Security Officer-Investigator's
(ARSO-I) main foci. Since then Tel Aviv has
learned a great deal about the multi-million dollar
industry and its fraudulent activities. Of particular
concern is that the majority of the workers in this
industry are Israeli, whether they are B1B2 visa
holders, LPRs or dual American-Israelis; key
companies have told us that they prefer to hire
Israelis instead of Americans. Of late, the industry
has been using its KIOSK marketing experience to
branch out into related fields: hair straighteners,
hair extensions, hair accessories and other assorted
items such as other types of cosmetics, perfumes,
pillows, toys, wind spinners and even, roasted nuts.

The Dead Sea industry has spread to more than 36
states, creating a major presence across America.
This industry also operates in countries like
Australia, New Zealand, the UK, and Germany.
Unfortunately, its U.S. presence is not entirely
"clean," for there are known issues of B1B2 visa
holders working illegally; illegal worker
exploitation; no federal or local taxes being paid on

workers' earnings; filing applications for extensions and/or changes of status as a means of continuing illegal work; bogus marriages to keep key staff in the United States; B1 in lieu of H3 letter and H3 visa scams; non-transparent corporate structures established to create distance from illegal workers; transport of huge sums of cash
to Israel suggesting organized crime and money laundering; as well as an increased number of real estate ventures that suggest the same. Moreover, it is culturally acceptable for post-army Israelis to work illegally in the United States; key parts of the Dead Sea industry have been able to base a large part of their business models upon the employment of illegal workers.

These issues and other important topics of concern will be delineated in this lengthy background cable. The unifying factor is that all of these issues have wider implications. Aside from the criminal aspects of this fraud, a key implication is the increased visa revocation/refusal and denial of entry rates for post-army Israelis, which among other things, complicate Israel's high-profile desire to join the Visa Waiver Program. Contact information for readers who wish to receive e-mail updates is available at the end of this cable. END SUMMARY

2. (SBU)Known B1H3 letter drafters (Israel-based) are:

STS (majority user and has several TECS records), AK Global Investments and Management LLC, KIT, Gaya Inc, Global Spa LTD, Ela Marketing LLC, Tal Yosifun LTD, JNS Global Israel LTD, Sol Enterprise Israel LTD, Market Trade LTD, Mor Universal Management Consultants, and Global Market Trade LTD (formerly JG Cosmetics LTD). [NOTE: Gaya Inc and Sol Enterprise Israel LTD have residential addresses.]

(SBU) Known US counterparts to above Israeli companies:

A&B United, Coral Cosmetics, E-Marketing, Enias
Beauty, Everesteam, Feel Free LLC, Gill
Cosmetics, Gizbo Trading, JNS Global, Lali
Beauty (aka Cart Planet), Libra LLC, LMD 4
Florida, Lucidity Enterprises, Mall Security
Enterprises, MDS, Micaella, Nine DEC, Sound
Creation, Spa to Go (MI), Stanga and Suns Inc.

3. --------------------------------
Dead Sea and Organized Crime (OC)

(SBU) Organized Crime in the Dead Sea industry is
a real concern. Tel Aviv has consistently received
information that large sums of money are allegedly
being laundered and transported between the
United States and Israel. Due to the amount of
money being laundered and transported, Tel Aviv
has long suspected a link between the Dead Sea
industry and OC. In early December, FPU received
an e-mail from an informant who said he had
information alleging that a key Dead Sea company
is connected to OC. ARSO-I and FPU subsequently
interviewed this informant; the ARSO-I's report of
this interview states: "The SUBJECT stated that
s/he is in possession of computer disks with all of
this company's accounts, money totals, smuggled
bulk cash from the United States to Israel
and has a complete understanding of the alleged
illegal activities to include the employing of illegal
workers, suspected drug smuggling, money
laundering, intimidation, threats, extortion, and
tax evasion. The SUBJECT also claimed that this
company is allegedly owned by a major organized
crime family in Israel that has
threatened SUBJECT'S life, extorted money from
SUBJECT, and has sent people to physically
assault SUBJECT." Due to the ongoing criminal
investigation in the United States, no additional
details can be released at this time.

46.(SBU)Further adding credibility to our
suspicions, is an arrest case from this past summer
in Japan where KIOSKs run by young Israelis were
allegedly being used by an OC organization to

219

launder its drug money and real estate investment deals. As noted above, some Dead Sea companies have real estate and investment companies as part of their overall structure.

47. (SBU) Shell and holding companies are all part of the industry's corporate strategy, designed mainly to distance themselves from the illegal workers at the KIOSKs. To exemplify, one Dead Sea holding company has 60+ companies under it. Now, assume that one of those 60+ companies has a contract with another company and that other company then hires the illegal workers. This scenario is quite common, complicating our efforts to combat and uncover Dead Sea fraud. Furthermore, once a company is found to be employing illegal workers it merely changes its name or creates a new owner for a shell company and applies for H2B petitions. As mentioned earlier, there are a handful of attorneys who have been filing the majority of the Dead Sea industry's petitions and I539s. They appear to be passionate lobbyists for these new companies--almost as if there had been a previous working relationship (as in, with the "old" company).

48.(SBU) Sometimes, key Dead Sea players have been "caught-out" by their own non-transparent corporate structures. Recently, Tel Aviv received an e-mail complaint from one of the known Dead Sea lawyers that also included the CEO's angry e-mail to that lawyer. Problem: that CEO had, in theory, nothing to do with the petitioning company as he was the CEO of a different company. FPM investigated and discovered that the CEO's company sub-leases the KIOSKs to the petitioning company. Furthermore, the CEO's company has a TECS record that says it doesn't exist.

49.(SBU) As a side note: Tel Aviv FPU has a large and growing list of known OC figures identified through open source materials and confirmed by

ARSO-I through Israeli Law Enforcement sources. Tel Aviv FPU and ARSO-I are working with the Legal Attach on possible strategies to combat OC in conjunction with FPU's revocation of visas for convicted OC members.

HEADER VZCZCXYZ0008
RR RUEHWEB

DE RUEHTV #0140/01 0250537
ZNR UUUUU ZZH
R 250537Z JAN 10
FM AMEMBASSY TEL AVIV
TO RUEHC/SECSTATE WASHDC 5076
INFO RUEHRO/AMEMBASSY ROME 8617
RUEHJM/AMCONSUL JERUSALEM 3571
RHMFIUU/DEPT OF HOMELAND
SECURITY WASHDC

Chapter 10 -- Mossad target: the Port of Houston

The busy port of Houston may have been the location of a second major terrorist attack on America involving Mossad. The suspicions surround the April 2008 shooting death by Houston police of a longtime CIA asset named Roland "Tony" Carnaby.

Carnaby was the President of the Houston chapter of the Association for Intelligence Officers (AFIO), an association of former CIA and other intelligence officers. He was involved in monitoring Israeli firms moving money and goods in and out of Israel.

Carnaby was gunned down in an April 29 "hit' by two Houston police officers. The investigation surrounding the shooting was rife with inconsistencies. The Houston Police Department originally misidentified one of the policemen involved in Carnaby's slaying as "Charles Foster." It was later discovered that Charles Foster was actually Cecil Foster. A Charles Foster had previously retired from the Houston police force.

Carnaby was also working with the Joint Terrorism Task Force in Houston, as well as the CIA's Counter-terrorism Center (CTC) in attempting to beef up security for the Port of Houston. Carnaby was involved in conducting security surveys of the port and discovered that the Department of Homeland Security had tolerated gaping holes in port security.

Carnaby and Houston intelligence and law enforcement personnel were also investigating the presence of "Middle Easterners" who were conducting surveillance of the Port of Houston. The "Middle Eastern" designator is the term used by the FBI for Israelis in order to avoid "political" problems with superiors.

The word from the federal agents who were involved in identifying weaknesses in Houston port security is they did not want to see "another 9/11-type *part false flag*."

Carnaby was a longtime player in Houston area intelligence matters and had established a close relationship with former President George H. W. Bush.

Carnaby's Lebanese family, which used the original spelling of Karnabe, is very well-respected by different political and religious factions in the country. Carnaby had stumbled across some significant intelligence impacting the overall situation in the Middle East and that at the time of his death Carnaby wanted the intelligence to personally reach CIA director Michael Hayden without delay. Carnaby also understood that the CIA and FBI had been infiltrated by gatekeepers who were ensuring that critical intelligence did not reach top U.S. policy makers in intelligence and law enforcement.

The Houston police report on Carnaby's shooting listed his address as 1302 Waugh Drive, Number 475, Houston. The address is a UPS Store and 475 is a mail box number. The address was used for Carnaby's non-official cover (NOC) firm, Carnaby Shipping Company, Ltd. Carnaby's security work with the CIA and Houston's Joint Terrorism Task Force involved the Port of

Houston and Houston area airports. Carnaby maintained two mail boxes at the UPS Store.

Carnaby's UPS Store mailing address

Carnaby was not only close to former CIA director George Tenet but had cultivated close ties to members of Mossad. According to a colleague, Carnaby said he maintained contact with Mossad agents because he believed in "keeping one's friends close, but one's enemies even closer."

A copy of Tenet's book contained an inscription by Tenet to "Tony" that was verified as Tenet's signature and handwriting.

According to a U.S. intelligence source, there was also a concerted effort by Carnaby's enemies to tarnish his image and bona fides in a "carefully orchestrated effort": to create a false CIA persona in order to damage Carnaby's own actual record as an agent.

The lawsuit complaint filed by Carnaby's widow against the Houston police states that Carnaby "died of a gunshot wound to the back which caused fatal loss of blood."[132]

The Houston police impounded Carnaby's laptop computer, which contained details on a CIA non-official cover (NOC) network tasked with protecting U.S. and foreign ports from terrorist attacks and the smuggling of weapons of mass destruction (WMDs).[133]

Carnaby was a frequent user of the CIA disguises designed and developed by Antonio (Tony) and Jonna Mendez, both of whom served as the CIA's "masters of disguise." The husband and wife team co-authored the book *Spy Dust: Two Masters of Disguise Reveal the Tools & Operations That Helped Win the Cold War.* They also spoke at the Association for Intelligence Officers gala event in Houston on Sept. 1, 2007, an event presided over by Carnaby. Tony, known as "Q" within the CIA, and Jonna were reputedly close friends of Carnaby.

Carnaby, according to US intelligence sources, was a user of the Mendez disguises, particularly in the Middle East. On one occasion, Carnaby was dressed as a Jordanian street cleaner in Amman while surveilling a target. Carnaby spoke the Jordanian dialect of Arabic perfectly. A few hours later, the "street cleaner" was clad in a blue blazer and sun glasses in Amman, operating under U.S. intelligence cover.

In addition to speaking Arabic dialects, including Levantine, Egyptian, and Yemeni, Carnaby could also speak fluent Hebrew and he maintained close links to Israeli intelligence

---

[132] May 14, 2008, "CIA agent kept Mossad 'close,'" WayneMadsenReport.com
[133] May 20, 2008, "Carnaby had access inside the Israeli Prime Minister's office," WayneMadsenReport.com

agents and assets abroad and in Houston. He was concerned that as with "two CIAs," there was also "two Mossads" in operation, one official and the other a dangerous rogue operation.

Carnaby's Texas Concealed Handgun License denoted the category "SA," meaning "Special Agent," a code that appears on the permits of law enforcement and intelligence officers in Texas, including CIA, FBI, and DEA agents. The Houston police who stopped Carnaby clearly saw this code on his permit.

Associates of Carnaby said that he worked in Laos during the Indochina conflict with long-time CIA clandestine agent Ted Shackley. It is believed by some of his CIA colleagues that Carnaby's age was older than his reported 52. It is common for CIA agents to claim different ages to avoid identification from public records.

There would be further intrigue in Texas concerning suspected Israeli agents.

Retired CIA sources in Texas confided that 2011 break-in of the Bexar County Court House in San Antonio was not the work of a few drunk French nationals, said to be of Moroccan descent, but part of a larger intelligence operation directed against the United States by a foreign intelligence service, reportedly that of Israel.

Although they broke into a court house and were, allegedly, French citizens of Moroccan descent, charges against three of the five "tourists" were dropped by Bexar County Magistrate Judge Amalia 'Molly' Cavazos. The decision puzzled the Bexar County Sheriff's office and the county district attorney's office.

The October 19, 2011, incident at the Bexar County Court House also worried U.S.

Representative Henry Cuellar, a member of the House Homeland Security Committee. Cuellar KSAT-TV in San Antonio that the night before the "French" nationals broke into the court house, a Turkish national was detained for suspiciously taking photographs of the old main post office building, which is next to the Alamo. Like the French nationals, the Turkish national was said to be a tourist.

Sources believe the presence of the "French" nationals in the court house was related to the nearby GEOINT Symposium, billed as the nation's largest annual intelligence event, at the Henry B. Gonzalez Convention Center was related to the operations of the team at the court house.

It was learned by the author that law enforcement and U.S. intelligence are prohibited from arresting and bringing charges against Israeli intelligence agents in the United States, even if the agents are found to be involved in operations that impact on U.S. national security and threaten the safety of American citizens. To pursue Israeli intelligence operations, against an unwritten prohibition, is for an FBI or CIA agent to sign his or her own professional death sentence, with a charge of "anti-Semitism" sealing the fate of anyone who dares challenge the "hands-off" policy on Israeli agents.

The following information was received from a veteran U.S. intelligence source in Texas:

"Too many unanswered questions. The charges against the three were dropped by a Magistrate Judge even before the search of the RV was completed. I can't help but wonder if they installed some type of listening devices inside of the court house. Also, if it is the court house that I am thinking of, there is a direct line of sight to the Henry B. Gonzalez Convention Center. If it is that specific court house then they could have easily installed a micro-transmitter capable of intercepting signals intelligence from the National Geospatial Intelligence Convention somewhere in the court house, which has yet to be discovered. Their computers would have the requisite receivers and they could have lingered in the area and picked up intelligence from the convention center. I also find it interesting that the charges were dropped by a Magistrate Judge before the RV was searched and before the computers could have been gone through. The five are probably on their way to whatever their next destination is.

It is a long drive from NY JFK to Miami to pick up one person. Where did they stop on the way? Why did they drive to Miami instead of one person getting a flight from MIA to JFK? How long did it take the four to get to Miami from JFK? When did they make their reservations for the RV in New Jersey? Why did the Feds back off and leave the case to the Bexar County Prosecutor? The Feds could have put a "hold" on the 5 or at a minimum the three. The only conclusion that one can reach is that there are multiple unanswered questions that even a minor league Intel officer would pursue. Did the FBI put GPS tracking on their RV? If not, why not? Nothing about this case stands up to any scrutiny. If three regular people were caught breaking into the exact same Court House they would face charges of 'Breaking and entering,' 'Burglary' or 'Criminal Mischief,' but they would not have all charges dropped. I would be interested if they are being tracked via GPS that could yield a lot of information and prove what they are really up to. No reason not to track them in the first instance."

Israel appeared to have learned a lesson from past intelligence exposures on U.S. soil. By

228

using nationals of France and Turkey, both of which have an ample number of sayanim, Jewish collaborators for Israeli intelligence, Israeli consular officials can avoid the diplomatic and public relations fallout, such as what arose after arrests across the country of Israeli "art students," "movers," and mall kiosk vendors. Instead of Israeli diplomats with egg on their faces, that fell to French and Turkish consular officers in Texas. There was also the odd report that the French consulate in Dallas was contacted to handle the matter of the five burglars at the San Antonio Court House. However, the French are represented in Dallas by an Honorary Consul, hardly the sort of individual who would get involved in a potential criminal matter involving French nationals. France maintains a full consulate in Houston.

The five French nationals arrested claimed not to be conversant in English, however, they were all proficient in English. Israelis, when arrested, often claim to not understand English, which results in a delay in interrogations until Israeli diplomatic officials can bail them out.

The following was also from intelligence sources in Texas: "This district for U.S. District Courts [Hipolito F. Garcia Federal Building and U.S. Courthouse, Southern District of Texas] has more CIA operatives in it than anywhere else in Texas outside of Houston. I am told that. St. Mary's Law School in San Antonio is a major player in security and terror. In reading this story, couple the highest ranking Mossad spy in Texas with that program at St. Mary's."[134]

---

[134] October 25-26, , "San Antonio court house break-in has

229

***

New York City and Houston, one carried out and the other never conducted by Mossad, were not the only Israeli terrorist operations carried out on U.S. soil.

According to a former investigative reporter for CBS News, who spoke to the author on background, the bombing of the Alfred P. Murrah Federal Office Building on April 19, 1995 was the result of a closely coordinated plot by domestic espionage assets of Israel's Mossad and a German intelligence asset to pin blame for the bombing on Arabs in the United States and link the attack to Iraqi President Saddam Hussein.

The official conclusion of federal prosecutors were that Army veteran Timothy McVeigh and his colleague Terry Nichols were solely to blame for the bombing that killed 169 people, including 19 children, and was, at the time, the deadliest terrorist attack ever to be carried out on American soil. The FBI ruled out any foreign connections to McVeigh and Nichols. McVeigh was executed by lethal injection after his conviction on 11 federal counts on June 11, 2001. Nichols was sentenced to life in prison for his role in the bombing.

The CBS News source tracked McVeigh to a right-wing and outwardly anti-Semitic "Christian Identity" compound known as Elohim City, Oklahoma and a German intelligence officer named Andreas Strassmeier, who spoke Hebrew and who had been married to an Israeli national. Strassmeier had infiltrated the Elohim City group.

---

national security ramifications," WayneMadsenReport.com

Strassmeier was the son of Gunther Strassmeier, the chief of staff to German Chancellor Helmut Kohl.

What soon became obvious to the CBS News source was that Strassmeier was the tip of a plot to blow up the Murrah buildng that involved not only a German intelligence asset, Strassmeier, but Israel's Mossad and key officials in the FBI and Bureau of Alcohol, Tobacco and Firearms (BATF).

The source also confirmed that a prison inmate named Kenny Trentadue, who was being held at the Federal Transfer Center for prisoners in Oklahoma City and who was mistaken by FBI interogators as the mysterious "John Doe number 2" accomplice of McVeigh, was beaten to death in the federal facility on August 21, 1995, two days after the Murrah bombing. Trentadue was arrested on the Mexican border on June 10, 1995, for driving on a suspended license. The source said the FBI concocted a story that Trentadue had committed suicide even though there was forensic evidence that he had been beaten to death.

In the days after the Murrah building bombing, a number of Arab-Americans were detained and questioned by federal authorities until it was announced that the bombing was carried out by right-wing elements to avenge the government's siege of the Branch Davidian compound in Waco, Texas two years before.

Although the Strassmeier and Israeli connection to Oklahoma City was delved into by elements of the European media, the story never saw the light of day in the U.S. corporate media and much of the details have been relegated to Internet web sites.

Israeli false flag attacks on U.S. targets continue to this day and appear to be the rule rather than the exception. On March 23, a Yemeni court sentenced one man to death and two others to prison sentences for spying for Israel. The three Yemenis, including their Mossad-run leader, Bassam Abdullah al-Haidari, were said to have volunteered their services directly to Israeli Prime Minister Ehud Olmert, who accepted. The group established a false flag group called the "Islamic Jihad of Yemen," which claimed to have bombed the U.S. embassy in Sana'a last September, killing 18, including six attackers. Six Islamic Jihad of Yemen suspects were arrested in October 2008 and three were released due to lack of evidence.

The Israeli involvement in the attack on the American embassy in Yemen is the latest in a long history of attacks on U.S. targets by the Mossad that were made to look like they were carried out by Arabs. In 1968, King Hussein of Jordan accused Israel of being behind the group Kateb al Nasr, which staged a stone attack on the U.S. embassy in Amman that resulted in widespread violence that caused the deaths of 29 people. Hussein said Jordan had fallen victim to "another Lavon affair," a reference to a 1954 Mossad attack on the U.S. Information Service library in Cairo that was made to appear that it was carried out by Egypt. The operation was organized by Israeli Defense Minister Pinhas Lavon.[135]

---

[135] March 25-26, 2009, "Oklahoma City bombing was a Mossad-German intelligence operation," WayneMadsenReport.com

In subsequent years, Mossad was linked to Islamist terrorist groups from Ansar al-Sharia, which was linked to the 2012 attack on the U.S. diplomatic compound in Benghazi, Libya to the Islamic State of Iraq and the Levant (ISIL), which carried out terrorist attacks on U.S. citizens, as well as religious and ethnic minorities, including Christians, Yazidis, Kurds, Turkoman, Shi'as, Alawites, and Sunnis in the Iraq-Syria region.

Chapter 11 -- Learning Lessons

It has been said over and over again that nations do not have friends but only interests. Israel's actions against the United States, which is claims is its closest allies, have never reflected the actions of a "friend."

While the presence of Saudi-funded terrorist cells in the United States has been reported by the corporate media, the same cannot be said about the presence of Israeli terrorist cells in America.

A knowledgeable source with close ties to senior Department of Justice officials told the author that the suspicious activities of young Israeli men and women who aggressively push Israeli cosmetic products at mall kiosks around the United States is not only tied to gathering intelligence from nearby military and government facilities but also to recruit American Jews for specialized "counter-terrorism" training at a Jewish training camp in the Catskills in upstate New York.

According to the well-placed source, retired and reserve members of the Israel Defense Force (IDF) are conducting paramilitary training at the Catskills camp. The camp once belonged to the Jewish Defense League (JDL), a designated terrorist organization in the United States. Israeli Foreign Minister Avigdor Lieberman was once a follower of Rabbi Meir Kahane, the founder of the JDL and the outlawed racist Kach Party in Israel. Many Kahanists openly celebrated the assassination of Prime Minister Yitzhak Rabin in

1995. Rabin's assassin, Yigal Amir, was associated with the Kahanists/Kachists and a former Mossad chief once told this editor that the fingerprints on the first assassination of an Israeli Prime Minister went right up the chain to Binyamin Netanyahu, the current Israeli Prime Minister.

Today, the IDF training of militant Jews is conducted under the aegis of Kitat Konenut (KK), which is self-described as a "non political, non partisan team of freedom loving Americans devoted to teaching preparedness against terrorism and natural disasters," adding, "Kitat Konenut trains with veterans of the Israel Defense Forces and incorporates elite Israeli fighting skills."

Although it claims non-partisanship, the KK's heroes are all Israeli terrorists, including Zionist fascist leader Zeev Jabotinsky; Avraham (Yair) Stern, the founder of the Jewish terrorist Stern Gang, and first Likud Prime Minister and one-time terrorist Menachem Begin. In fact, the Catskills camp is also sometimes referred to as "Camp Jabotinsky" and has been linked to the Jewish Defense Organization, a spin-off of the JDL.

The extreme-Zionist KK claims to have a close working relationship with the New York City Police and Fire Departments. KK also has a Los Angeles unit that claims members within the Los Angeles Police Department.[136]

---

[136] July 27, 2009, "About those Israel mall vendors: kiosks providing cover for IDF training of militant Jews in United States," WayneMadsenReport.com

There were some loyal U.S. law enforcement and intelligence officials who tried to warn about the threat from both the Israeli and Saudi sides of the joint Saudi-Israeli 9/11 terror plot. Many of them paid with their careers.

A case in point is FBI agent Michael Dick who aggressively pursued the Israeli movers in New Jersey after 9/11.

Former FBI Special Agent Michael Dick is not the person one would suspect would be suing his old employer for damages resulting from a series of what Dick believed were a volley of retaliatory measures. Dick was not only a 17-year veteran of the FBI but an Army reserve officer who saw duty in some of the most dangerous areas in America's battle against terrorists.

Michael Dick was a colleague of the late FBI chief of the New York Joint Terrorism Task Force John O'Neill. O'Neill was hired as a security officer for the World Trade Center days before the buildings were struck on 9/11. O'Neill died in the collapse of the North Tower.

In his aggressive pursuit of Al Qaeda, O'Neill, according to people who worked closely with him, began to have serious concerns over complicity by those inside the Clinton and Bush administrations. There was the mysterious theft in the summer of 2000 of his briefcase at a Tampa hotel during a retirement seminar where the only other participants were 150 other FBI agents. In the briefcase were a few classified emails and a classified document called the Annual Field Office Report, a summary of the New York FBI's office counter-terrorist and counter-intelligence operations, including one very sensitive investigation being conducted by another New

York counter-intelligence FBI special agent, Special Agent Dick. Although a lighter, cigar cutter, and expensive pen were stolen, the papers were all accounted for when the briefcase turned up 90 minutes later at another nearby hotel. Ninety minutes, of course, was sufficient time to photocopy the documents and discover what O'Neill knew about both Al Qaeda and their Israeli shadows.

Special Agent Dick, who worked closely with O'Neill, had discovered a troubling ring of Israeli movers operating in the New York and New Jersey areas. Furthermore, some of these Israelis not only had connections with Mossad and other Israeli intelligence agencies but were also shadowing Arab and Muslims that had been under investigation as potential terrorist cells. But the Israelis were acting independently and there was no effort made to inform the FBI or local police of any intelligence they were obtaining on their targets.

COMPLAINANT LN PO-DeCarlo   FN Scott   DOB
Address   Ph.

    Prior to the transportation to the State Police facilities this officer
was told without question by the driver "We are Israeli, We are not your
problem. Your problems are our problems, The Palestinians are the problem."
I was also told by Mr. Yaron Shimuel "We were on the west side highway during
the incident." The black bag that the driver was fumbling with contained all
of his belongings (see attached Receipt from the FBI for its contents).
Mr. Oded Ellner was in possession of a white sock like sack filled with $4,700
in cash (see attached receipt from FBI).
This officer did not speak to the Special Agent in charge Kevin Donovan and
there were many other agents involved in the investigation. Two of which were
Dan O'Brien (973) 792-3389 and Robert F Taylor Jr.(973)792-3327.

East Rutherford police report on arrest of five Israelis seen celebrating as first plane struck World Trade Center on 9/11. The Israelis tried to blame 9/11 on the Palestinians. Not one Palestinian was involved in the 9/11 attack.

Further frustrating Dick's counter-espionage

activities against the Israelis was the fact that they were using communications methods that made it almost impossible to conduct communications surveillance: they used Verizon pre-paid cell phones, two-way Nextel walkie-talkies, and Internet cafes.

At the same time, the DEA had discovered a nationwide ring of Israeli "art students," many of whom had past connections to Israeli intelligence and military demolition units, were operating in and around New York and New Jersey. What the DEA did not realize was that the art students were also shadowing the very same Arab cells that would later carry out the 9/11 attacks.

Dick was a first responder at the scene of the World Trade Center conflagration on September 11. His law suit against Attorney General Eric Holder, former FBI director Robert Mueller, and "other unknown defendants" states: "SA Dick was a first responder to the attacks on the World Trade Center on September 11, 2001. He saw dead bodies, charred remains and the horrendous physical damages and human loss caused by the collapse of the twin towers. SA Dick also watched helplessly as people from the Towers plummeted to their death."

URBAN MOVING SYSTEMS INC.

888•MOVES•US (888•668•3787)
Info@urbanmoving.com

Weehawken NJ 201-558-0210 3-18th St. Weehawken, NJ 07087
New York NY 212-664-1268 446 W50th St. NY,NY 10019

WWW.URBANMOVING.COM

Dick's law suit describes his other work for the FBI:

"Dick also spearheaded efforts to investigate the abduction of Wall Street Journalist Daniel Pearl. Mr. Pearl was brutally beheaded by Khalid Sheik Mohammed. SA Dick helped track leads on the murder of Mr. Pearl and worked on several other highly classified terrorist attack cases. When the Diplomatic enclave in Islamabad, Pakistan was attacked and a church bombed, SA Dick responded to the church and saw the carnage that ensued when a suicide bomber detonated a number of grenades during a church service, which killed twenty-five people. SA Dick stayed in Pakistan on dangerous counterterrorism cases at great personal risk. He assisted in the return of a kidnapped Pakistani girl whose father was close to President Pervez Musharraf."

The law suit further states: "In 2004, Special Agent Dick was promoted to Supervisory Special Agent. Among his duties was coordinating information received on potential terrorist threats. As part of his duties, SSA Dick was assigned to secure information from the Motley Rice Law Firm, which represented the families of 9-11 victims, who were pursuing a civil law suit against high ranking Saudi Arabian officials and bankers . . . SSA Dick was to collect information from the Motley Firm, but was not to disclose any information from the Bureau. SSA Dick scrupulously followed this policy. The flow of information was one way from the families' attorneys to the Bureau.

Private investigators hired by the Motley Firm pursued investigative leads outside the United States, without being subject to the limitations imposed on government, federal law enforcement, the military or corporations on informants for federal agencies. The investigations led to the capture of a high level terrorist and a reward was given by the Department of Justice in the millions of dollars to the persons who assisted in that capture . . . An investigator hired by the Motley Rice Firm, Michael Patrick Jost, because disgruntled when he was denied a portion of that award. Mr. Jost blamed SSA Dick for being excluded from the award. Mr. Jost began a campaign to malign SSA Dick with allegations that he had passed sensitive information to the families of victims of the September 11, 2001 terrorist attacks and was receiving compensation from their attorneys. Mr. Jost began a fanciful tale of how SSA Dick had amassed riches as a result of using his FBI position for private gain."

Dick learned that he had been fingered in an investigation as a result of Jost's contact with the FBI. However, it should also be stated that Dick remained on the radar screen of groups like the American Israel Public Affairs Committee (AIPAC) as a result of the knowledge he possessed of Israel's culpability in the 9/11 attack.

Dick's law suit explains the background to the FBI's allegations against him:

" In October 2005, Mr. Dick was mobilized by the U.S. Army as part of Operation Enduring Freedom. He served in combat operations until 2008. In April, 2006, while on active duty in the United States Army, Mr. Dick was informed that he was the subject of a criminal investigation based on Mr. Jost's allegations. The FBI commenced an investigation. For two years, in

240

2005 and 2006, the Inspector General of the Department of Justice conducted a lengthy inquiry into Mr. Jost's allegations. The IG determined that no criminal wrongdoing or violation of the Department of Justice policy occurred and declined the matter. In the spring of 2007, Mr. Dick was informed he was cleared by the OIG investigators of criminal misconduct."

Believing the IG had cleared him, Dick was surprised to learn that the matter was still being pursued by the FBI. The law suit states:

"The matter was then apparently referred to the FBI Office of Professional Responsibility (OPR), which delayed action until November, 2007. On November 26, 2007, the FBI proposed SSA Dick's dismissal contenting that he used improper investigation techniques, was derelict in his duties, disclosed classified or sensitive information and lacked candor under oath in responding to the Inspector General's inquiry. At the time it proposed the dismissal, SA Dick was on active duty. The FBI contacted the Army regarding the proposed termination, as the proposal also led to Mr. Dick's security clearance being suspended . . .

The Army then discharged Mr. Dick from active duty in April, 2008 based on the suspension of his security clearance, he remained a reservist.

OPR continued to conduct a prolonged two year investigation from 2007-2009. Mr. Dick opposed the proposed removal. In his opposition Mr. Dick meticulously attacked both the unauthorized disclosure allegation and the purported wrongfulness of sending the loan. [The loan was to a former FBI agent to pay for transport out of a dangerous area]. For example, in his defense, Mr. Dick pointed out that he had simply made a loan to a former Special Agent who was serving as a private contractor in the Middle East. That individual, with whom Mr. Dick has worked closely, called Mr. Dick to advise him his cover had been compromised and he could be killed. The individual pleaded for an immediate $10,000 loan to secure transport, Mr. Dick gave him the loan to protect him from capture, torture and death.

As to the alleged unauthorized disclosures, Mr. Dick pointed out that he had been authorized to send the communications he did on pre-approved electronic systems by his supervisor, who had full prior knowledge of his conduct. He also pointed out that he had direct, actual supervisory approval for the manner in which the information was sent.

On April 29, 2008, FBI OPR determined that while Mr. Dick had not lacked candor and was not derelict in his duties, he nevertheless disclosed "sensitive information" and used 'improper techniques.' OPR contended Mr. Dick wrongfully used a private service to send sensitive information and improperly provided $10,000 to the civilian contractor. OPR mitigated the proposed termination to a 40 day suspension. Mr. Dick appealed the matter internally to the Disciplinary Review Board (DRB). The DRB is an internal appeal unit which applies a reasonable basis standard to its review. So long as OPR's decision is reasonable, the DRB will not disturb the findings.

On November 3, 2008, the FBI, through its DRB, made a final determination. The Board determined that OPR's finding on the most serious charge of disclosure of sensitive information was incorrect and that Mr. Dick provided proof of supervisory review and approval of his actions. As to the alleged improper loan, the Bureau found that while Mr. Dick had loaned money to a private investigator working overseas for the 9/11 families, in alleged contravention of a then existing Bureau policy regarding such loans, his motivation was to protect the life of the investigator who needed to leave the Middle Eastern country where he was working immediately or face capture, torture and death. Again, this investigator was a former FBI Agent.

The DRB also determined that that Mr. Dick made a *de minimis* administrative error in communications with Patrick Jost, when they discussed a protected source of information. The finding was made although Mr. Jost was already aware of the source, because the source had, themselves, made the disclosure of their status to Mr. Jost. The Bureau imposed a thirteen day suspension for the purported misconduct. Mr. Dick then appealed the suspension to the MSPB. A jurisdictional claim was raised since the suspension was less than fourteen days and the MSPB generally lacks the authority to hear appeals from suspensions of less than 14 days. Prior to the resolution of the issues, the parties settled the case. Mr. Dick believed the issues with the Bureau were finally at rest."

It is important to note that Dick's "Catch 22" back-and-forth with the FBI mirrors the same sort of administrative warfare conducted by U.S. intelligence agencies that have targeted employees for retaliatory measures based on the information they acquired in the course of carrying out their tasks, especially information concerning 9/11 and the false intelligence that led to the U.S. invasion of Iraq.

Dick's travails with the FBI were only just beginning. From his lawsuit:

"In January, 2011, SA Dick was interrogated by FBI investigators primarily on the same allegations raised by Patrick Jost that led to the prior disciplinary action. The interview occurred although Mr. Dick protested the interrogation. At the interrogation he claimed he was being denied due process and his right to have a representative present. The FBI had its own counsel participate in the interview.

In May, 2011, Special Agent Dick returned to active duty service with the U.S. Military. Mr. Dick was, at the time a Lieutenant Colonel assigned to Counter Terrorist Operations in the Special Operations Command. Mr. Dick remained on active duty service until August, 2011 when he was abruptly released. The FBI had contacted the U.S. Army and advised the Army that Mr. Dick was under investigation and that the military should 'flag' him and his clearance. A 'flag' represents notification of a limit on the official's access to classified information. Since Mr. Dick's Army position required classified access, the imposition of a flag ended Mr. Dick's career and voided his pending promotion to Colonel. The U.S. Army discharged Mr. Dick from active duty and assigned him to the Inactive Ready Reserves. Mr. Dick returned to the FBI in August, 2011. He was initially told he would not be rehired. When

Mr. Dick threatened to bring a claim under the Uniformed Services Employment and Reemployment Rights Act (USERRA), he was reinstated."

For Dick, there was no end to his problems with the FBI:

"On the same day he returned, SA Dick was informed he was subject to a new FBI OPR investigation, which largely consisted of same stale charges arising from the prior OPR action initiated in 2006. The Bureau also contended that SA Dick had violated FBI policy by maintaining a blind trust to pay for his prior legal defense. Such a move was obviously designed to punish Dick for opposing the Bureau and to intimidate any future legal representative or effort by Mr. Dick to raise funds for a legal defense. The Bureau, over the next two years, demanded information that went to the core of Mr. Dick's relationship with attorneys at Holland and Knight and Joseph Smith, a private attorney, who had assisted Mr. Dick. The Bureau contended, without any citation to legal authority of any kind that Mr. Dick had committed fraud when his attorneys had agreed privately and separately to give him a portion of the Agency's award of attorney's fees to his counsel Joseph Smith."

Dick protested that the FBI gained knowledge of privileged client-attorney communications:

"Mr. Dick protested that an agreement between him and his prior counsel over a reduction in fees and a return of a portion of those fees back to Mr. Dick was both privileged and not indicia of fraud. He stated there was no fraud because the Agency had agreed to pay the fees and that any agreement between Dick and his counsel about how to use those fees was privileged. There was and is no 'fraud.' The Agency agreed to pay a certain amount as part of a settlement. How Mr. Smith chose to use those funds is a matter between him and Mr. Dick. Mr. Dick argued that his attorney's decision to reduce his own award and give a portion of it back to Mr. Dick was a private agreement that did not secure government payment through fraud. Further, Dick appropriately declared any payment he received on his income tax statements. The FBI has never stated what it determined with respect to these allegations despite the passage of 20 months, nor has it; despite repeated requests cited any law that would render such a payment fraudulent or at all illegal. The FBI has demanded and received, under protest, Mr. Dick's tax returns, his communications with his counsel and additional financial information because the Bureau had threatened to discipline Mr. Dick if he did not comply.

Mr. Dick has never received any discipline from this second investigation nor has he been cleared of the charges. The FBI has simply maintained that he is under investigation since January 2011 to the present day. The duration of the investigation is extraordinary and troubling from several perspectives. If Mr. Dick had engaged in actionable misconduct, the Bureau's delay in taking action is inexcusable since the Bureau had a duty to punish that misconduct appropriately. Mr. Dick believes the investigation is designed to actually never end and is merely a retaliatory tool."

The FBI continued to harass Dick and the time frame of the personnel actions against Dick matches the Obama administration's incessant harassment of a number of national security whistleblowers, including the National Security Agency's former employees Thomas Drake, William Binney, Russ Tice, and Kirk Wiebe; the Central Intelligence Agency's Jeffrey Sterling; the State Department's Peter Van Buren; and a others, in addition to pressure by the Justice Department on *The New York Times's* Jim Risen to reveal his national security sources.

Dick's problems with the FBI grew increasingly more difficult. These problems culminated on May 7, 2013, when after suffering an injury while at the Quantico, Virginia FBI firing range, a series of events ended up with the FBI telling Fox News that Dick was suspected of going on a rampage and that FBI headquarters in Washington was his target. The story was bogus but the damage was done. Dick's story of retaliation for "knowing too much" about 9/11 is not unique. Officials of dozens of federal, state, and local agencies, as well as private businesses, have similar harrowing tales.

Only when those who tell the truth about governmental criminal conspiracies, even those that touch on Israel and Saudi Arabia, are treated properly as whistleblowers are dealt a fair hand, will the United States begin to recover from the horrors brought on by 9/11.

INDEX

About the Author

Wayne Madsen is a Washington, DC-based investigative journalist, author and syndicated columnist. He has written for *The Village Voice*, *The Progressive*, *Counterpunch*, *In These Times*, and *The American Conservative*. His columns have appeared in *The Miami Herald*, *Houston Chronicle*, *Philadelphia Inquirer*, *Columbus Dispatch*, *Sacramento Bee*, and *Atlanta Journal-Constitution*, among others.

He serves as the editor of the WayneMadsenReport.com, an "Inside-the-Beltway" news and views website.

Madsen is the author of *The Handbook of Personal Data Protection* (London: Macmillan, 1992), an acclaimed reference book on international data protection law; *Genocide and Covert Operations in Africa 1993-1999* (Edwin Mellen Press, 1999); co-author of *America's Nightmare: The Presidency of George Bush II* (Dandelion, 2003); author of *Jaded Tasks: Big Oil, Black Ops & Brass Plates*, *Overthrow a Fascist Regime on $15 a Day.* (Trine Day), *Manufacturing of a President: The CIA's Insertion of Barack H. Obama, Jr. into the White House* (Amazon Create and Lulu Press), and *L'Affaire Petraeus: The Benghazi Stand-Down and the Plot to "Carterize" Obama* (Lulu Press).

Madsen has been a regular contributor on RT. He has also been a frequent political and national security commentator on Fox News and has also appeared on ABC, NBC, CBS, PBS, CNN, BBC, Al Jazeera, and MS-NBC. Madsen has taken on Bill O'Reilly and Sean Hannity on their television shows. He has been invited to testify as a witness before the US House of Representatives, the UN Criminal Tribunal for Rwanda, and a terrorism investigation panel of the French government.

As a U.S. Naval Officer, he served in anti-submarine warfare, telecommunications, and computer

252

security positions. He subsequently was assigned to the National Security Agency. Madsen was a Senior Fellow for the Electronic Privacy Information Center (EPIC), a privacy advocacy organization.

Madsen is a member of the National Press Club.